BOOKS BY CLARENCE BROWN

BOOKS BY W. S. MERWIN

SELECTED POEMS

OSIP MANDELSTAM
SELECTED POEMS

translated by
Clarence Brown
and
W. S. Merwin

NEW YORK
ATHENEUM
1974

The following poems were originally published in
The New Yorker: 121, 304, 308 and 395.

English translation copyright © 1973 by Clarence Brown and W. S. Merwin
All rights reserved
Library of Congress catalog card number 73-81725
ISBN 0-689-10583-5
Manufactured in the United States of America by
Halliday Lithograph Corporation
West Hanover, Massachusetts
First American Edition

INTRODUCTION

Osip Emilievich Mandelstam was born in Warsaw in January
1891, but his family removed so soon thereafter to the imperial
Russian capital, St. Petersburg, that it became, in every meaning
of the term save the literal one, his native city. His father was a
leather merchant whose ancestors came from Kurland. His
mother, born Flora Verblovskaya, was a relative of the famous
literary historian Vengerov and prided herself on her family's
belonging to the intelligentsia. She herself was a teacher of
music, a love of which the most gifted of her three sons inherited.
The very fact of their residing in Petersburg testifies to the
privileged status of Mandelstam père, for Jews were permitted
to do so only exceptionally.

We know little of Osip Mandelstam's childhood aside from
what he himself recorded in his autobiographical work *The Noise
of Time*. True to its title, it concentrates more on the time than
on the young intelligence that was taking it in. But one carries
away much more from reading these deliberately blurred and
impressionistic pages than a sense of Russia's mauve decade.
Writing at a time when there was little left for him to celebrate
in the contemporary city, when the very name of Peter's capital
had already undergone the change through Petrograd to Lenin-
grad, he celebrated those images and events—the general 'noise'
of a culture now dead—that he retained in his mind, and it is
from these that we can piece together some notion of his early
years. It is a notion made up of contradictions that are un-
resolved—perhaps unresolvable.

On the one hand there is all the melancholy paraphernalia of
the 'dying age'—the 'unhealthy tranquillity and deep provincial-

ism' as Mandelstam put it, and the note of decay is one of the constants of the book; but on the other hand, it is all depicted with such stylistic brio, with such relish for the somehow festive aplomb of Petersburg's going down, accompanied by eternal concerts and military parades as counterpoints to the funeral pomps, that the impression left is that of indelible joy. Upon all of this he knew himself to be looking as an outsider, an onlooker from what he called 'the Judaic chaos' of his family and its traditions:

> But what had I to do with the Guards' festivals, the monotonous prettiness of the host of the infantry and its steeds, the stone-faced battalions flowing with hollow tread down the Millionnaya, gray with marble and granite? All the elegant mirage of Petersburg was merely a dream, a brilliant covering thrown over the abyss, while round about there sprawled the chaos of Judaism—not a motherland, not a house, not a hearth, but precisely a chaos, the unknown womb world whence I had issued, which I feared, about which I made vague conjectures and fled, always fled.

Was it not, then, even more of a triumph that he should so have possessed the Czar's capital and made it his own? Beside such paragraphs one must set the rest of the book: the string of French and Swiss governesses who succeeded one another in the nursery, sedate games in the Summer Garden, the treasures of Russian literature—Pushkin in calico binding and 'heavy' Dostoevsky— as furnished by the family bookcase, the music of Tchaikovsky and Scriabin, concerts by Hofmann and Kubelik, the fine sand of a Finnish summer resort, Vera Komissarzhevskaya's theater, and a richly particular gallery of human portraits. On balance, one's final impression of his childhood is that he spent it savoring experience in an atmosphere that afforded him sufficient emotional security and a certain clarity of self-definition. The contrary assumption would make it more difficult to understand that strength of character that sustained Mandelstam through the tragic years that were to come.

It is a further testimony to his family's standing that he gained admission to the Tenishev School, an academy that managed to be not only thoroughly elite but also doctrinairely 'democratic' and educationally very advanced. Vladimir Nabokov's liberal father would send the future great novelist to the same school some ten years later (to leave memoirs of it predictably different from those of Mandelstam); and another Jew who managed to be admitted, Victor Zhirmunsky, would become one of Russia's greatest scholars and a loyal friend of his classmate Mandelstam for the rest of his life. It was a hotbed of excellence.

From there he went abroad on the first of several trips to study and travel in France, Italy, and Germany. His formal courses during a semester spent at Heidelberg in 1909–1910 included lectures on the philosophy of Kant and on Old French. On his return to Petersburg he entered the University, though he never received his degree. The very fact of his having been accepted as a student was baffling for years, for a Jew could be admitted only with the very highest academic credentials, and though Mandelstam had greatly profited from the Tenishev School, his actual record there was very indifferent. His widow recently revealed that he had undertaken to be baptized a Lutheran somewhere in Finland purely for the sake of being matriculated as a Christian. In later life his attitude toward religion in general and Christianity in particular would have forbidden so lightly considered a step, to which he subsequently attached little importance.

By 1913, the year when *Stone*, his first book of poems, appeared, Mandelstam was already known within the confines of the Petersburg literary world as a poet of unusual promise. Still, the little green brochure struck his contemporaries as a kind of revelation. It was something of a mystery where he had come from. The reigning school was that of Russian Symbolism, which included Alexander Blok, Mandelstam's nearest competitor as Russia's greatest twentieth-century poet, and also Andrey Bely, Valery Bryusov, Konstantine Balmont, Vyacheslav Ivanov, Zinaida Gippius, and a great many others. There is a sense, indeed, in which Symbolism included at one time or another *all* the other poets of Russia's 'Silver Age' on either side of the century mark, for it furnished an indispensable part of their education, and its significance therefore greatly exceeds that of its several successors.

But this brief introduction is hardly the place for polemics, and besides, there are many who find it genuinely consoling to assign individual genius to a multiplicity of 'schools'. Let us stick to the prevailing categories.

Symbolism, then, which had arisen at about the time of Mandelstam's own entrance into the world, was now, on the arrival of his first book, defunct as a unified movement. At the end of the last century it had provided a crash course in poetic re-education after Russian nineteenth-century verse, languishing under the overpowering success of Russian nineteenth-century prose, had seemed at times to aspire to prose itself, or else to retreat into the mere prettiness of numbers. By the end of the first decade of this century, the original Symbolist impulse towards reform of taste and technique had become fragmented and drained off into various neo-Romantic dead-ends such as diabolism, an exaggerated absorption with the ego of the poet, various embarrassing forms of the occult and mystical religion, and, in general, a sort of hankering after the drastic for its own sake. Younger poets coming into their maturity at this time inherited the Symbolist rejuvenation of technique, but their elders' preoccupations in other fields left them cold, and the only other schools of modern Russian poetry that deserve mention along with the Symbolists took their departure. Mayakovsky and Khlebnikov were 'Futurists'. Mandelstam was an 'Acmeist'.

I doubt that the programme of Acmeism, as originally formulated, could ever be arrived at purely by means of induction, on the evidence of the poems alone, for the poets who gathered for a time under its banner were very different one from the other. The leader was Nikolay Gumilev, and the only other poets of any lasting consequence were Gumilev's sometime wife, Anna Akhmatova, and Mandelstam himself. The number of poems by these people which, independently of all overt pronouncements, might reasonably be compared on the basis of their formal and thematic resemblance, so as to evince a distinctly separate movement in poetry, is not large. Put in a few words, the Acmeists' early declarations boil down to a desire for poems free of any Symbolist nonsense about contact with other worlds. Images were to be concrete and sharply realized and the statement of poems rigorously logical. Their strength, like that of Antaeus, was to come from contact with the earth. Gumilev in particular called for a virile, even feral, outlook on life and for a steady, wholesome equilibrium in all things, but especially in the construction of poems. For a notion of what Acmeism was or supposed itself to be, it is tempting to send the English reader to a source much closer to home: Ezra Pound's list of 'Don'ts for Imagists'.

For it is hardly feasible to send him directly to the poems translated here. Indeed, from reading the majority of these poems either in Russian or in English one is more likely to conclude that most of the early tenets of Acmeism had been devised for the express purpose of being ignored by Mandelstam. The fact is that he had his own view of Acmeism, and it is a view that only partly coincides with that outlined above. It also evolved over a long period of time, during which it changed. In 1910 in an essay on François Villon he had already sketched an Acmeist poetic that antedated the later and better known formulations of others. In 1937 Akhmatova reports him as having replied to some heckler demanding a definition of Acmeism that it was 'a homesickness for world culture'. This exhausted, defiant retort was his last word on the subject, but it carries, of course, a good deal more emotional than theoretical weight. In between these dates he found occasions for more extended and reasoned deliberations, the last fully composed of which appears in an essay of 1922, where Mandelstam's Acmeism emerges as half poetics and half moral doctrine. He now called it, revealingly enough, by a new name—the 'organic school'. While it is naturally not possible to treat the full complexity of his thought here, the reader of the following pages will need to know at least this: that the 'logic' so insistently called for by the syndics of the movement has now far more to do with the intuitive and purely verbal logic of inner association—with the logic, say, of Mallarmé—than with the rather commonsense logic of discursive statement to be found in Gumilev. As for the moral component of Mandelstam's Acmeism, that might without undue distortion be put as a kind of democratic humanism, which does not differ greatly from what the Acmeists always, explicitly and by inference, desired.

However one resolves the question whether Acmeism or any other -ism ever existed except on the paper of its manifestoes, it is clear that Acmeists existed, for that is what they were called by themselves and others. They were a group of poets, most of them young and unfledged at the time, who clustered around the commanding personality of Gumilev. When the latter enlisted for the World War, which he did at the first opportunity, he left the group with no natural center, and that was the end of Acmeism in its public and least arguable form—their frequent gatherings to read and discuss their own work. Mandelstam was not conscripted, and of course did not enlist, but he did engage in various home-front activities such as organizing benefit evenings of poetry. *Stone* appeared in a second, expanded edition in 1916.

The deprivations of the War and the Revolution frequently drove Mandelstam to the more tranquil and well-provided south of Russia, especially to the Crimea. Returning to the north at the end of the Civil War, he brought with him a new book, *Tristia*, which was published in 1922. It was the book of a poet who had passed through the schooling of the Symbolists, testified to by the early poems of *Stone*, and the more doctrinaire formulations of primitive Acmeism, to achieve a voice uniquely his own. Mandelstam looked over the heads of his immediate preceptors, as it were, to Derzhavin (1743–1816) and Tyutchev (1803–1873), poets who combine exquisite verbal power with a ceremonious, even oratorical, solemnity of manner. The following year, 1923, both his collections of poetry were brought out in new editions and he was now a poet of considerable and widespread fame. He was also married. His wife, Nadezhda Yakovlevna, is now herself known throughout the world for her moving memoir of their last years together, published in English translation as *Hope Against Hope* (1970). It is chiefly owing to her that our knowledge of Mandelstam's subsequent life is infinitely fuller and more exact than that of his former life.

It became increasingly difficult for him to make a living—not that it had ever been easy. But now the causes were different.

Like practically all the intellectuals of Russia, Mandelstam had welcomed the Revolution, but from a very early time he had also mistrusted the Bolshevik usurpers of it, as had most of the other Acmeists. Gumilev's life had ended before one of the firing squads of the new regime in 1921, and all his former associates were automatically suspect. Employment began to depend more and more upon one's being certifiably loyal, and Mandelstam, who took few pains to conceal his real feelings, was flagrantly not so. Editors of journals and publishing houses were increasingly warned to be on their guard against printing the work of the class enemy. In 1928 Mandelstam published three separate books: *Poems*, which contained his previous two collections plus the poems written between 1921 and 1925; *On Poetry*, his collected critical essays; and *The Egyptian Stamp*, his collected prose. That would make the year seem to be the summit of his career so far, but the appearance is very deceptive. For some three or four years before that he had been forced to live by writing children's books, by doing hack translations and journalism, and by whatever odd jobs he could pick up in the government publishing houses. His standing among connoisseurs of poetry had never been higher, but the Soviet state viewed him with increasing suspicion and malevolence.

In spite of this, he had a very highly placed protector in the person of Nikolay Bukharin, who liked Mandelstam and valued his poetry. It was only through his intervention that Mandelstam survived a plot that was meant to remove him altogether from the profession of letters. In the same year (1928) when three of his own books appeared, Mandelstam brought out Charles de Coster's *Thyl Ulenspiegel*, which he had been commissioned by a government publishing house to edit on the basis of two existing Russian translations. When it appeared, however, Mandelstam's name was printed on the title-page as *translator*. This provided the grounds for a campaign of vilification against him in the press. One of the translators all but accused him of plagiarism, and attacked the editorial work itself as slovenly and inaccurate. To readers in the West this may all seem very small potatoes, but it is necessary to remember, first, that Russian polemics can reach a level of personal invective so outrageous as to be almost literally intolerable, and second, that public defamation of character was only the preliminary step in a series that would end, as Mandelstam foresaw, with his exclusion from the right to publish at all. Furthermore, where his personal honor was concerned, Mandelstam was as touchy as Pushkin. The accusations against him, which were after all merely the public culmination of a long series of private affronts, drove him to paroxysms of rage. Bukharin finally had the campaign stopped and arranged for Mandelstam and his wife to be sent off to distant Armenia, ostensibly for the purpose of reporting on how that country was enjoying sovietization but actually to be out of harm's way. This worked, but the shock of what he had endured during the last years of the Twenties dried up the sources of his poetry for an agonizing period of five years—his 'deaf-mute' period, as he called it. On the way back from Armenia in 1930 he cured himself by a desperate act of self-therapy: a strange and completely unclassifiable work known as *Fourth Prose*. A blend of autobiography, criticism, and sheer excoriation, it is Mandelstam's summation of his defense against all the forces that seemed bent on silencing him. Poetry returned, and so did another work of prose (this one publishable, which in Russia *Fourth Prose* never has been), a work called *Journey to Armenia*. Heavily censored, it appeared in a journal in 1933, the last time that his work would appear in the Soviet press for some three decades of 'non-existence'.

The story of Mandelstam's final years, thanks to his widow's obstinate courage and her own extraordinary powers as a writer, is now widely known. He was arrested in 1934 for having composed a poem in which he made grim fun of Stalin, the 'Kremlin mountaineer', and his relish for torture and execution (see page 69). Someone informed on him and he was immediately clapped into prison, where he underwent intensive interrogation and psychological and physical torment. Friends intervened in so far as they dared or were able—his protector Bukharin was to be among the first victims of Stalin's purge later in the decade—and by some miracle the intervention worked. The poet was not shot, as everyone reasonably supposed that he would be, but exiled, first to a small town in the Urals (where, half insane from the prison experience, he attempted to kill himself) and later on in the provincial town of Voronezh. His wife was at his side from the moment he was put on the train into exile, and her presence literally kept him alive through his remaining years, for his anxiety in her slightest absence was so great as to threaten nervous and physical collapse. They lived on the donations of friends, for the most part. The bouts of mental suffering seem to have been even worse than the physical deprivations; Mandelstam lived in the expectation of imminent peril.

It would be natural to imagine that the poems composed at this period would all be haggard replicas of his experience, but this is not so. There are nightmares of colossal atrocities— 'mounds of human heads'—on a scale befitting the actual crimes of Stalin. But the visitations of poetry were occasions far too sustaining and joyous for Mandelstam to derive no more from them than that.

> Opulent poverty, regal indigence!
> Live in it calmly, be at peace.
> Blessed are these days, these nights,
> and innocent is the labor's singing sweetness.

The 'labor' was that of poetry, and in the employment of his art Mandelstam took what, in the light of his circumstances, one is tempted to call an incorrigible delight. There was his favorite bird, the goldfinch, its colors and attitude, to be turned into words, or a boy on a sled, or a Breughel-like winter scene. It was not from mere self-indulgence that his pleasure arose, for Mandelstam, like every Russian poet worthy of the name, felt that his gift imposed upon him an obligation: the people needed poetry no less than bread.

> The people need poetry that will be their own secret
> to keep them awake forever,
> and bathe them in the bright-haired wave
> of its breathing.

The term of exile expired in May 1937, and the Mandelstams returned to Moscow only to find that they had lost the right to 'living-space' upon which Nadezhda had maintained a tenuous hold. Homeless and unable to find work, the following twelvemonth is a nightmare of wandering and terror: the wave of second arrests, as they were called, was under way. Mandelstam's condition worsened. He had two heart attacks. Finally, in May 1938, they received the visitors whom they had long expected. Mandelstam's sentence 'for counter-revolutionary activities' was five years of hard labor (he had been seized at a rural sanatorium where he was recuperating). Held for a while in prison, he was put in the autumn on one of the prisoner trains that were then plying between European Russia and its remote eastern regions. He seems to have been quite insane at times, though there were lucid intervals. It must have been during one of these that he wrote a last letter in October, 1938, a scrap of brown paper asking to be sent warm clothes and money and saying that he was being held at a transit camp pending shipment to a permanent one. Alexander Mandelstam received notice that his brother had died—of 'heart failure'—on 27 December 1938.

AN AFTERTHOUGHT ON THE TRANSLATION

It was my intention, and hope, that the foregoing should suffice as a minimal introduction to the poet whose altered voice fills the following pages. The publisher—and, even more cogently, my co-translator—have now convinced me against what may yet prove to have been my better judgment that many readers of such a volume as this will be legitimately curious as to how it came into being. Hence this brief word concerning not so much the voice that was there to be altered, nor yet its altered form, but the process of alteration itself.

For more years than I find it comfortable to admit I have been preparing a study of Mandelstam's life and poetry (now to be published by Cambridge University Press under the title *Mandelstam*), and in the course of that I developed a habit of preparing worksheets on each poem. These included, along with notes on every aspect of the poem that struck me, notations of variant readings, semantic nuances of the diction, peculiarities of the prosody, and so on, a plain English translation, often with numerous alternative translations. Thus, when W. S. Merwin proposed to me in the spring of 1971 that we might collaborate on an English translation of Mandelstam (Russian, by some inadvertance, having been omitted from his impressive array of languages), it struck me that much of my own share of the work had already been done. This proved, though only very partially, to be true, for the first stage in our work was my simply turning over to Merwin my worksheets. From these, with a truly heroic effort of decipherment, he produced first versions. In the intervening couple of years we have, with a pleasure that I trust was mutual, debated the early results, sometimes syllable by syllable, often by painstaking correspondence and more often still by personal meetings in Princeton and London. Bargains were struck, but no compromises were undertaken, I hope, with the English poem that was trying to be born out of Mandelstam's Russian.

The poems that resulted are of course no longer *calques* of the original (though an occasional happy line or two from the worksheet did sometimes survive), but we have not consciously invented thoughts or images that the original could in no sense warrant. It need scarcely be said, I suppose, that we never considered the folly of trying to convey to the ear of our English readers the sounds of the Russian.

Here is an example that will perhaps save much explanation. The beginning of the Russian original of No. 394 might be brought over into a painfully literal English as follows:

Limping automatically [or involuntarily] on the empty earth
with [her] irregular, sweet gait,
she walks, slightly preceding
[her] quick girlfriend and the youth one year older [or
    younger] than she.
The straitened freedom of [her] animating affliction
draws her [on].

xv

And it seems that a lucid surmise
wants to linger in her gait—
[the surmise] that this spring weather
is for us the first mother [i.e., Eve] of the grave's vault
and [that] this will be forever going on.

I am of course unable, and have no desire, to enquire into what
passed through Merwin's mind as he wrestled with something
like the above (and he is, by the way, blameless for this Introduc-
tion), but most literate readers, I think, could account for the
clock that does not occur in Mandelstam's poem. It is a concrete
image (very Mandelstamian, by lucky chance) that *tells* in the
line as one of those limp adverbs would not, and its tick can be
discerned in the *quick* and *back* later on. Why is it her left leg? I
suppose because I told Merwin that the particular verb for limp-
ing normally occurs in a phrase specifying *which* leg is lame, and
I see from the worksheet that I have noted that Natasha Shtempel,
to whom the poem was written in 1937, is in fact lame in her *left*
leg. I spent several delightful days with this now aged lady in
1966 and think I know what Mandelstam meant by 'sweet', but
the word has inconvenient overtones in English—at least for
Merwin. It strikes me that 'drags at her foot' is a marvellous
visual and kinetic image for the rather cerebral sense of the literal
version (there is an entirely different excellence in the Russian,
where the cerebral thought is beautifully concretized by lines
that do not so much describe as *enact* Natasha Shtempel's way of
walking). The repetition of 'she must know' strikes me as
effective in this general context of dire periodicity. There is noth-
ing in the Russian to account for it other than the dire periodicity,
though it occurs to me that my having had to repeat 'surmise'
for the sake of the sense might have helped to prompt it. But it is
pointless to go on praising Merwin's superiority—not over the
original, but over the exiguous sense remaining from it on my
worksheet. One final note: 'go on' results from an altered read-
ing (in the first, now superseded, edition of Vol. 1 of the New
York edition, the Russian word meant 'begin').

Would Mandelstam approve? I cannot quite bring myself up

to the presumption of answering in his name, so I shall rather let him answer for himself by an account of his own practice.

Mandelstam also translated. Like most of the Russian poets who brought about the great reflowering of their art around the turn of the century, he was at home in the languages of culture, and translation was a part of his response to the world. With the advent of the bad times that I have mentioned, when his own work was being systematically rejected by 'vigilant' editors, he was driven to translating in order to live. He had to translate under sweatshop conditions, the texts assigned him being the trash in vogue at the time with the authorities. This loathsome hackwork even crowded out his own muse. He had to endure reading here and there in official reference works, chronicles of the literary scene and so on, that he had given up poetry and 'gone over to translating', a legend that clung to his name for years.

But even under these conditions he sometimes managed to translate in response to the old genuine urgency—out of love. In 1933 he turned four sonnets of Petrarch into Russian. They remained unpublished and indeed unknown until the late Victor Zhirmunsky, his old Tenishev classmate, gave them to me in 1962, whereupon they came out in the New York edition of his works. I had received the texts alone, with no indication of where the originals might be among Petrarch's hundreds of sonnets, so my first concern was naturally to seek these out. It was an awful headache. No sooner would I have identified this or that image in an opening line or two than some wild divergence would convince me that Mandelstam must have been working from another original. The 'other original' stubbornly refusing to turn up, I was driven back to my starting point, and had to conclude what is the point of this little narrative: that Mandelstam had translated Petrarch not into Russian, but into Mandelstam.

Lest any reader think that by lending myself to this undertaking I have switched sides in the Lowell–Nabokov debate, let me say, first, that he should inspect my several tributes to Nabokov, and secondly, that that controversy, now that time had dissipated the fog of animus, can be seen for what it was, a pseudo-controversy. Lowell does not translate into English, but into Lowell; Nabokov can be said to translate into literal English only by those who will accept his definition of literal English: in reality, it is Nabokov. Merwin has translated Mandelstam into Merwin. When one is speaking of writers of the stature of Lowell, Nabokov, and Merwin, this strikes me as being the happiest of situations.

I can imagine, if only just, an English poem that might reproduce what one critic has called the 'cello sound' of this or that poem by Mandelstam or some other of its effects—its rhymes, its plastic sculpture of rhythm, its tenuously resonating change-ringing on some syllabic bell, its abrupt syntactic somersaults, and all the rest. What is more, I can imagine the only audience that might, or should, appreciate this English poem: a roomful of native Russians who, with the original itself unfolding in their mind's ear, have just enough English to collate the two, and approve the result. They would approve it, happily unaware of the exorbitant price that had been paid, and consequently as happily unable to assess its merit as an English poem of our own time.

We have tried to translate Mandelstam into the English that works as an instrument of poetry in our own time, and we have accepted the responsibility entailed in the fact that to translate is to change. Those of my colleagues in the academy who are sent up the wall by 'mistakes' in the translation of poetry, those who are happy to maintain that poetry is untranslatable here on earth, and the arbiters of their own brand of literalism everywhere, have probably by now read far enough in this book.

Clarence Brown
Easter 1973, Princeton

NOTE ON THE TEXT

The Russian text and the numbering of Mandelstam's poems come from his *Sobranie sochinenii* (Collected Works), Vol. I (2nd, ed., revised and expanded, 1967) ed. Gleb Struve and Boris Filippov, with introductions by Clarence Brown, Gleb Struve, and E. M. Rais. New York: Inter-Language Literature Associates.

The poems numbered 92, 112, 113, and 119 were translated by W. S. Merwin and Olga Carlisle and are reprinted from W. S. Merwin, *Selected Translations 1948–1968* (New York, 1968).

\

FROM *STONE*

I

The shy speechless sound
of a fruit falling from its tree,
and around it the silent music
of the forest, unbroken . . .   1908

2

Christmas trees burn in the forest with gilded flames,
toy wolves glare from the bushes—

O my prophetic sadness,
O my calm freedom,
and the dead crystal vault of heaven laughing without end!

                                                  1908

3

All the lamps were turned low.
You slipped out quickly in a thin shawl.
We disturbed no one.
The servants went on sleeping.   1908

24

Leaves scarcely breathing
in the black breeze;
the flickering swallow
draws circles in the dusk.

In my loving
dying heart
a twilight is coming,
a last ray, gently reproaching.

And over the evening forest
the bronze moon climbs to its place.
Why has the music stopped?
Why is there such silence? 1911

37

THE LUTHERAN

As I was out walking I met a funeral,
last Sunday, by the Lutheran church,
and I stayed idly attending
the stern grief of the faithful.

None of the words of their language came through.
Nothing gleamed but the thin bridles
and the dull glint of the horseshoes, reflected
on the street empty for Sunday.

But in the rocking dusk of the hearse
where the dummy sadness had retired
the autumn roses lay in their buttonhole
without a word or a tear.

Foreigners in black ribbons came walking behind
beside the women weak with weeping,
veils drawn across red faces.
The implacable coachman kept moving on.

Whoever you were, vanished Lutheran
don't worry, it went off well.
The proper tears dimmed the proper eyes,
the right bells rang through the autumn.

And I thought plain thoughts, as was fitting.
We're not prophets nor apostles.
Hell has no fears for us, we repent for no Heaven.
Our candles make a twilight at noon.   1912

47

He can't speak, and we can't bear it!
It's like watching a mutilation of the soul.
A reciter stood on the stage, wild-eyed,
and they went mad, shouting 'Please, please!'

I knew that another was there, invisible,
a man from a nightmare, reading 'Ulalume'.
What's meaning but vanity? A word is a sound—
one of the handmaidens of the seraphim.

Poe's harp-song of the House of Usher. Then the madman
swallowed some water, came to himself, was silent.
I was in the street. The silk of autumn was whistling . . .

                                                        1913

'Ulalume': a poem by Edgar Allen Poe (1847).
l.9: the reference is to Poe's short story 'The Fall of the House of Usher' in his
Tales of the Grotesque and Arabesque (1840).

48

THE ADMIRALTY

In the northern capital a dusty poplar languishes.
The translucent clockface is lost in the leaves,
and through the dark green a frigate or acropolis
gleams far away, brother of water and sky.

An aerial ship and a touch-me-not mast,
a yardstick for Peter's successors, teaching
that beauty is no demi-god's whim,
it's the plain carpenter's fierce rule-of-eye.

The four sovereign elements smile on us,
but man in his freedom has made a fifth.
Do not the chaste lines of this ark
deny the dominion of space?

The capricious jellyfish clutch in anger,
anchors are rusting like abandoned plows—
and behold the locks of the three dimensions are sprung
and all the seas of the world lie open.   1913

54

Poison in the bread, the air drunk dry.
Hard to doctor the wounds.
Joseph sold into Egypt
grieved no more bitterly for home.

Bedouins under the stars
close their eyes, sitting their horses,
and improvise songs
out of the troubles of the day.

No lack of subject:
one lost a quiver in the sand,
one bartered away a stallion . . .
the mist of events drifts away.

And if the song is sung truly,
from the whole heart, everything
at last vanishes: nothing is left
but space, the stars, the singer.   1913

60

The horse-shoes still ring
with the old days.
The doormen sleep on the counters
like bales of furs.

And the porter, weary as a king,
hears knocking at the iron gate,
gets up yawning like a barnyard—
they've waked the old Scythian!

So Ovid with his waning love
wove Rome with snow in his lines,
and sang of the ox-cart
in our wild wagon-trains.   1914

62

Orioles in the woods: length of vowels alone
makes the meter of the classic lines. No more
than once a year, though, nature pours out
the full-drawn length, the verse of Homer.

This day yawns like a caesura: a lull
beginning in the morning, difficult, going on and on:
the grazing oxen, the golden langor powerless
to call out of the reed the riches of one whole note.

1914

66

Let the names of imperial cities
caress the ears with brief meaning.
It's not Rome the city that lives on,
it's man's place in the universe.

Emperors try to rule that,
priests find excuses for wars,
but the day that place falls empty
houses and altars are trash. [1914]

78

Insomnia. Homer. Taut sails.
I've read to the middle of the list of ships:
the strung-out flock, the stream of cranes
that once rose above Hellas.

Flight of cranes crossing strange borders,
leaders drenched with the foam of the gods,
where are you sailing? What would Troy be to you,
men of Achaea, without Helen?

The sea—Homer—it's all moved by love. But to whom
shall I listen? No sound now from Homer,
and the black sea roars like a speech
and thunders up the bed. 1915

79

The old ewes, the black Chaldeans,
the spawn of night, cowled in darkness,
go off grumbling to the hills
like plebs annoyed at Rome,

in thousands, shuffling their
knees shaggy as bird-perches,
shaking and bounding in their foaming curls
like lots in a giant wheel.

They need their Caesar. They need their black hill,
the Rome of the sheep, with its seven hills,
and the barking of dogs, a campfire under the sky,
and the rank smoke of a hut and barn.

The bushes marched at them like a wall.
The tents of the warriors started to run.
They left in holy disorder.
The fleece hangs in a heavy wave.   [1915]

80

Herds of horses neigh happily in the meadows
and the valley has rusted as Rome did.
The transparent river bears away
dry gold: the spring days of the classics.

In autumn, in the wilderness, trampling
the oak leaves that have buried the paths,
I remember Caesar, the imperial features
like a woman's, from the side, with the nose of one
                              not to be trusted.

Capitol, Forum, are far away
from these colors draining peacefully out of the season.
Even on the rim of the world I can hear the time
of Augustus rolling away, an orb, an apple.

When I'm old, may even my sadness shine.
In Rome I was born, and it comes back to me.
My she-wolf was kind autumn,
And August smiled on me—the month of the Caesars.

1915

FROM *TRISTIA*

How these veils and these shining robes
weigh me down in my shame!

A famous disaster
is coming to stone Troezen,
the royal stairs
will be scarlet with shame.

. . . .

. . . .

and a black sun will rise
to light the mother's desire.

If it were only hatred that seethed in me—
but look, the truth opened its wings and left me.

Phaedra the black flame is burning
by day,
a torch for a death, for a burial
by day.
Hippolytus, beware of your mother:
Phaedra is the night watching you
by day.

I have stained the sun with my black love.
Pure death will be cold to the lips.

We are afraid. A queen
and we are afraid to grieve.
Goaded by Theseus,
the night struck him down,
and we are a dirge
going home with the dead
to chill the black sun
that raged and would not sleep.   1916

The two lines deleted by Mandelstam (indicated here by rows of dots) were
never restored.

to Marina Tsvetaeva

On a sled covered with straw.
Our own matting scarcely covered us.
We rode through wide Moscow
from the Sparrow Hills to a little church we knew well.

Children in Uglich play at knucklebones.
A smell of bread baking.
I am taken through streets bare-headed.
In the chapel three lighted candles.

Not three lights but three meetings,
one blessed by God himself.
There will be no fourth. Rome is far.
And He never loved it.

The sled drove along black ruts.
People coming back from their walks.
Thin muzhiks and cross old women
restless at the gate.

In the raw distance a night of birds rose.
The bound hands went numb.
They're bringing the Tsarevich. The body turns to ice.
They set fire to the straw.

1916

Marina Tsvetaeva (1892–1941), one of the greatest of modern Russian poets, left
Russia after the Revolution but returned in 1939 and hanged herself two years
later. She and Mandelstam were close for a time in 1916.
l.5: Dimitry, son of Ivan IV and rightful heir to the throne of Muscovy, was
killed in the town of Uglich. Boris Godunov was suspected of complicity.

SOLOMINKA

I

Solominka, when you can't sleep in the huge chamber,
when you lie awake under the steep ceiling
waiting for its indifference to descend
onto your eyelids that feel everything,

dry Solominka, little ringing straw
who sipped up the whole of death—it has made you gentle.
The little dead straw has broken. It was Solominka.
No, not Salomea. It was the dead one.

Sleep won't come, but things grow heavier.
There are less of them than there were. And what silence!
The pillows hardly show in the mirror.
The bed floats on a lake, on a glass.

But that's not Solominka, under the grave satin,
above the black Neva, in the huge chamber.
The twelve months are singing of the hour of death
and the blue air is a river pale with ice.

The breath of grave December is flowing.
The room fills with the whole weight of the Neva.
It's not Solominka, it's Ligeia, dying.
I have learned you, blessed words.

II

I have learned you, blessed words.
Lenore, Solominka, Ligeia, Seraphita.
The huge room is full of the whole weight of the Neva.
Blood runs pale-blue from the granite.

Grave December gleams above the Neva.
The twelve months sing of the hour of death.
No, that's not Solominka, under the grave satin,
the dry straw sipping the deadly peace.

In my blood Ligeia is December.
Her blessed voice is asleep in the lidded stone.
But pity killed Solominka—or Salomea.
Whichever it was will never return.   1916

The name Solominka is also the Russian word for 'a straw'.
stanza 6: Lenore is one of the pale maidens of Edgar Allen Poe (see 'The Raven'),
as is Ligeia (see the story of that name). Séraphita is the heroine (and sometimes
the hero) of Balzac's novel by that name, 1835. Salomea is the name of the
addressee of this poem, Princess Salomea Andronikova. For a full analysis of this
poem see Clarence Brown, *Mandelstam* (Cambridge University Press, 1973), pp.
237–44.

89

We shall die in transparent Petropolis,
before Persephone our queen.
When we sigh we swallow the air of death.
Every hour will commemorate our last moments.

Sea-goddess, stern Athena,
lift off your great stone helmet.
We shall die in transparent Petropolis,
where Persephone, not you, is the queen.   1916

l.1: Mandelstam, like some other poets (e.g. Derzhavin), occasionally refers to
St. Petersburg as Petropolis—'the city of Peter'.

90

With no faith in the miracle of resurrection
we wandered through the cemetery.
—You know, everywhere
the earth reminds me of those hills

. . . .

. . . .

where Russia breaks off
above the black desolate sea.

A wide meadow falls away
under the monastery.
I wanted to stay in the plains
of Vladimir, and not go south,
but to linger in that dark wooden
colony of holy fools
with that foggy nun
was to wall myself up in trouble.

I kiss your sunburnt elbow
and a place on your wan forehead
which I know has stayed white
under the strand of dark gold.
I kiss your hand, the white
band the bracelet left.
The blazing summer of Taurida
performs miracles such as these.

How quickly you tanned,
and came to the Savior's poor icon,
and kissed without stopping,
you who were proud in Moscow.
The name is all that's left to us,
a miraculous sound.
Here, take this sand that I pour
from one palm to another.   1916

Mandelstam never added the lines indicated here as missing.

91

BLACK SUN

Nothing can erase this night
but there's still light with you.
At Jerusalem's gate
a black sun has risen.

The yellow one frightens me more.
Lullaby, lullaby. Israelites
have buried my mother
in the bright temple.

Somewhere outside grace,
with no priests to lead them,
Israelites have sung the requiem over her
in the bright temple.

The voices of Israelites
rang out over my mother.
I woke in the cradle, dazzled
by the black sun. 1916

92

The thread of gold cordial flowed from the bottle
with such languor that the hostess found time to say
here in mournful Tauris where our fates have cast us
we are never bored—with a glance over her shoulder.

On all hands the rites of Bacchus, as though the whole world
held only guards and dogs. As you go you see no one.
And the placid days roll past like heavy barrels. Far off
in the ancient rooms there are voices. Can't make them out.
    Can't answer.

After tea we went out into the great brown garden.
Dark blinds are dropped like eyelashes on the windows.
We move along the white columns looking at grapes. Beyond
    them
airy glass has been poured over the drowsing mountains.

I said the grape vines live on like an antique battle,
with gnarled cavalry tangling in curving waves.
Here in stone-starred Tauris is an art of Hellas: here, rusted,
are the noble ranks of the golden acres.

18

Meanwhile silence stands in the white room like a spinning
    wheel,
smelling of vinegar, paint, wine cool from the cellar.
Do you remember in the Greek house the wife they all loved?
Not Helen. The other. And how long she embroidered?

Golden fleece, where are you then, golden fleece?
All the way the heaved weight of the sea rumbled.
Leaving his boat and its sea-wearied sails,
Odysseus returned, filled with space and time.   1917

93

Far away is the gray
transparent spring of asphodels.
For the moment the sand still rustles,
in fact, the wave still seethes.
But here, like Persephone, my soul
enters the fortunate circle.
Such beautiful sunburnt hands as these
are not found in the kingdom of Hades.

Why do we entrust to a boat
the weight of the funeral urn,
and perform the black rose rite
over the amethyst water?
To the sea past Cape Meganom,
through the fogs, my soul is fighting;
a black sail will come back from there
after the burial.

How fast the unlighted bank
of storm clouds passes,
and under this windy moon
black rose petals are flying.
And that bird of death and grief,
the huge flag, memory,
trails from the cypress stern
a black border.

The sad fan of the past
opens with a hiss, toward the place
where the amulet was buried,
with a dark shudder, in the sand.
To the sea past Cape Meganom,
through the fogs, my soul is fighting;
a black sail will come back from there
after the burial.   1917

96

A hush that evening in the organ forest.
Then singing for us: Schubert, cradle songs,
the noise of a mill, and the voice of a storm
where the music had blue eyes and was drunk and laughing.

Brown and green is the world of the old song,
and young forever. There the maddened king
of the forest shakes the whispering crowns
of the nightingale lindens.

With darkness he returns, and his terrible strength
is wild in that song, like a black wine.
He is the Double, an empty ghost
peering mindlessly through a cold window.   1917

The clock-cricket singing,
that's the fever rustling.
The dry stove hissing,
that's the fire in red silk.

The teeth of mice milling
the thin supports of life,
that's the swallow my daughter
who unmoored my boat.

Rain-mumble on the roof—
that's the fire in black silk.
But even at the bottom of the sea
the bird-cherry will hear 'good-bye'.

For death is innocent,
and the heart,
all through the nightingale-fever,
however it turns, is still warm.   1917

101

A wandering fire at a terrible height—
can it be a star shining like that?
Transparent star, wandering fire,
your brother, Petropolis, is dying.

The dreams of earth blaze at a terrible height,
a green star is burning.
O if you are a star, this brother of water and sky,
your brother, Petropolis, is dying.

A giant ship at a terrible height
is rushing on, spreading its wings.
Green star, in splendid poverty
your brother, Petropolis, is dying.

Above the black Neva transparent spring
has broken, the wax of immortality is melting.
O if you are a star, Petropolis, your city,
your brother, Petropolis, is dying.   1918

103

THE TWILIGHT OF FREEDOM

Let us praise the twilight of freedom, brothers,
the great year of twilight!
A thick forest of nets has been let down
into the seething waters of night.
O sun, judge, people, desolate
are the years into which you are rising!

Let us praise the momentous burden
that the people's leader assumes, in tears.
Let us praise the twilight burden of power,
its weight too great to be borne.
Time, whoever has a heart
will hear your ship going down.

We have roped swallows together
into legions.
Now we can't see the sun.
Everywhere nature twitters as it moves.
In the deepening twilight the earth swims into the nets
and the sun can't be seen.

But what can we lose if we try one
groaning, wide, ungainly sweep of the rudder?
The earth swims. Courage,
brothers, as the cleft sea falls back from our plow.
Even as we freeze in Lethe we'll remember
the ten heavens the earth cost us.

Moscow. May 1918

TRISTIA

I have studied the science of good-byes,
the bare-headed laments of night.
The waiting lengthens as the oxen chew.
In the town the last hour of the watch.
And I have bowed to the knell of night in the rooster's throat
when eyes red with crying picked up their burden
of sorrow and looked into the distance
and the crying of women and the Muses' song became one.

Who can tell from the sound of the word 'parting'
what kind of bereavements await us,
what the rooster promises with his loud surprise
when a light shows in the Acropolis,
dawn of a new life,
the ox still swinging his jaw in the outer passage,
or why the rooster, announcing the new life,
flaps his wings on the ramparts?

A thing I love is the action of spinning:
the shuttle fluttering back and forth, the hum of the spindle,
and look, like swan's down floating toward us,
Delia, the barefoot shepherdess, flying—
o indigence at the root of our lives,
how poor is the language of happiness!
Everything's happened before and will happen again,
but still the moment of each meeting is sweet.

Amen. The little transparent figure
lies on the clean earthen plate
like a squirrel skin being stretched.
A girl bends to study the wax.
Who are we to guess at the hell of the Greeks?
Wax for women, bronze for men:
our lot falls to us in the field, fighting,
but to them death comes as they tell fortunes.   1918

l.20: Delia is a traditional name for the enamored shepherdess of pastoral poems.
The name occurs a few times in some of Pushkin's early lyrics.

108

Heaviness and tenderness—sisters: the same features.
Bees and wasps suck the heavy rose.
Man dies, heat leaves the sand, the sun
of yesterday is borne on a black stretcher.

Oh the heavy honeycomb, the tender webs—easier
to hoist a stone than to say your name!
Only one purpose is left me, but it is golden:
to free myself of the burden, time.

I drink the roiled air like a dark water.
Time has been plowed; the rose was earth. In a slow
whirlpool the heavy tender roses,
rose heaviness, rose tenderness, are plaited in double wreaths.
                                        Koktebel. March 1920

Venice, the stagnant, barren life—
it's plain what it means.
Look at it, peering with its cold smile
into the blue decayed glass.

Faint scent of leather. Fine veins in blue ink.
White snow. Green brocade.
They ride in cypress sedan chairs
and emerge from their cloaks, warm and dozing.

And candles still burn, burn, in baskets:
as if the dove had flown back into the Ark.
And on stage and among the listless assembly
man is dying.

For there's no way out of love and terror:
the ring of Saturn is heavier than platinum.
The block is draped in black velvet
and so is the beautiful face.

O Venice, the weight of your garments
and of your mirrors in their cypress frames!
Your air is cut in facets, and mountains
of blue decayed glass melt in the bedchamber.

A rose or a phial between fingers—
green Adriatic, farewell!
Why are you silent? Lady of Venice,
how can one escape this festivity of death?

The evening star flashes black in the mirror.
Everything passes. Truth is dark.
Man is born. Pearl dies.
Susanna will have to wait for the elders.   1920

III

FEODOSIA

In the ring of high hills
you stampede down your slope like sheep,
pink and white stones glistening
in the dry transparent air.
Pirate feluccas rock out at sea.
The port burns with poppies—Turkish flags.
Reed masts. The wave's resilient crystal.
Little boats on ropes like hammocks.

From morning till night, in every way possible,
everyone sings, grieving for a 'little apple'.
Its golden seed is borne away by the wind
and lost, and will never come back.
And promptly at nightfall, in the lanes,
the musicians, in twos and threes
bend and clumsily scrape
their improbable variations.

O little statues of Roman-nosed pilgrims!
O joyful Mediterranean bestiary!
Turks strut about in towels,
like roosters, by little hotels.
Dogs are moved in a small jail on wheels.
Dry dust blows in the streets,
and the vast cook from the battleship
looms cold-blooded above the market Furies.

Let's go where they've a collection of sciences,
and the art of making *shashlyk* and *chebureki*,
where the sign shows a pair of pants
to tell us what a man is.
A man's long coat, working without a head,
a barber's flying violin,
a hypnotized iron, a vision of heavenly
laundresses, smiling because it's difficult.

Here girls grow old in bangs
and ponder their curious garments.
Admirals in three-cornered hats
bring back Scheherazade's dream.
Transparent distance. A few grapevines.
A fresh wind that never drops.
And it's not far to Smyrna and Baghdad,
but it's a hard sail, and the same stars everywhere.

1920

112

When Psyche, who is Life, steps down into the shadows,
the translucent wood, following Persephone,
a blind swallow casts itself at her feet
with Stygian tenderness and a green branch.

The shades swarm to welcome the refugee,
their new little companion, and greet her with eager wailing,
wringing their frail arms before her
in awe and trouble and shy hope.

One of them holds out a mirror, and another, perfume,
because the soul is a woman and fond of trifles.
And the silence of the leafless forest is spotted
with transparent voices, dry laments, like a fine rain.

And in the fond confusion, uncertain where to begin,
the soul does not recognize the transparent woods.
She breathes on the mirror and she still clutches
the copper wafer, the fee for the misty crossing.   1920

I have forgotten the word I wanted to say.
A blind swallow returns to the palace of shadows
on clipped wings to flicker among the Transparent Ones.
In oblivion they are singing the night song.

No sound from the birds. No flowers on the immortelles.
The horses of night have transparent manes.
A little boat drifts on the dry river.
Among the crickets the word fades into oblivion.

And it rises slowly like a pavilion or a temple,
performs the madness of Antigone,
or falls at one's feet, a dead swallow,
with Stygian tenderness and a green branch.

Oh to bring back also the shyness of clairvoyant
fingers, the swelling joy of recognition.
I shrink from the wild grieving of the Muses,
from the mists, the ringing, the opening void.

It is given to mortals to love, to recognize,
to make sounds move to their fingers,
but I have forgotten what I wanted to say
and a bodiless thought returns to the palace of shadows.

The Transparent One still speaks, but of nothing.
Still a swallow, a friend known as a girl, Antigone.
The reverberations of Stygian remembrance
burn like black ice on one's lips.   November 1920

On the stage of ghosts a pale gleaming:
faint choirs of shades.
Melpomene has smothered the windows
of her house with silk.
Out in the courtyard the black camp
of carriages crackles with frost.
Long furs, everything shaggy,
hot snow sounding of teeth.

Servants sort bearskin coats
one by one from the piles.
One moth flies above many hands.
There's a rose under the furs.
Tiers of glittering fashionable insects
rise in the heat of the theater.
Out in the street little lights
flicker. Billows of steam roll in.

The coachmen have shouted themselves tired.
The crowd puffs and snores.
Ours is a cold winter, dear Eurydice.
Never mind. Sweeter to me
than the singing speech of Italy
is the language to which I was born.
Notes of remote harps well up in it
in secret.

Smoke hangs in the ragged sheepskins.
The street's black with drifted snow.
Out of the blessed singing height
immortal spring is flying to us
with the deathless aria:
—You will see green fields again;
the living swallow fell
on hot snow.   1920

l.3: Melpomene is the muse of tragedy.

Take from my palms, to soothe your heart,
a little honey, a little sun,
in obedience to Persephone's bees.

You can't untie a boat that was never moored,
nor hear a shadow in its furs,
nor move through thick life without fear.

For us, all that's left is kisses
tattered as the little bees
that die when they leave the hive.

Deep in the transparent night they're still humming,
at home in the dark wood on the mountain,
in the mint and lungwort and the past.

But lay to your heart my rough gift,
this unlovely dry necklace of dead bees
that once made a sun out of honey.   November 1920

There: the Eucharist, a gold sun,
hung in the air—an instant of splendor.
Here nothing should be heard but the Greek syllables—
the whole world held in the hands like a plain apple.

The solemn height of the holy office; the light
of July in the rotunda under the cupola;
so that we may sigh from full hearts, outside time,
for that little meadow where time does not flow.

And the Eucharist spreads like an eternal noon;
all partake of it, everyone plays and sings,
and in each one's eyes the sacred vessel
brims over with inexhaustible joy.   [1920]

We shall meet again, in Petersburg,
as though we had buried the sun there,
and then we shall pronounce for the first time
the blessed word with no meaning.
In the Soviet night, in the velvet dark,
in the black velvet Void, the loved eyes
of blessed women are still singing,
flowers are blooming that will never die.

The capital hunches like a wild cat,
a patrol is stationed on the bridge,
a single car rushes past in the dark,
snarling, hooting like a cuckoo.
For this night I need no pass.
I'm not afraid of the sentries.
I will pray in the Soviet night
for the blessed word with no meaning.

A rustling, as in a theater,
and a girl suddenly crying out,
and the arms of Cypris are weighed down
with roses that will never fall.
For something to do we warm ourselves at a bonfire,
maybe the ages will die away
and the loved hands of blessed women
will brush the light ashes together.

Somewhere audiences of red flowers exist,
and the fat sofas of the loges,
and a clockwork officer
looking down on the world.
Never mind if our candles go out
in the velvet, in the black Void. The bowed shoulders
of the blessed women are still singing.
You'll never notice the night's sun.

25 November 1920

I could not keep your hands in my own,
I failed the salt tender lips,
so I must wait now for dawn in the timbered Acropolis.
How I loathe the ageing stockades and their tears.

The Achaeans are constructing the horse in the dark,
hacking out the sides with their dented saws.
Nothing quiets the blood's dry fever, and for you
there is no designation, no sound, no modelled likeness.

How did I dare to think you might come back?
Why did I tear myself from you before it was time?
The dark has not faded yet, nor the cock crowed,
nor the hot axe bitten wood.

Resin has seeped from the stockade like transparent tears
and the town is conscious of its own wooden ribs,
but blood has rushed to the stairs and started climbing
and in dreams three times men have seen the seductive image.

Where is Troy, the beloved? The royal, the queenly roof.
Priam's high bird house will be hurled down
while arrows rattle like dry rain
and grow from the ground like shoots of a hazel.

The pin-prick of the last star vanishes without pain,
morning will tap at the shutter, a gray swallow,
and the slow day, like an ox that wakes on straw,
will lumber out from its long sleep to cross the rough haycocks.

                                                December 1920

At the hour when the moon appears in its city
and the wide avenues slowly fill with its light
then the night swells with bronze and sadness,
time the barbarian smashes the wax songs,

then the cuckoo counts her griefs on the stone tower
and the pale woman with the sickle steps down
through the dead, scattering straw on the board floor,
rolling huge spokes of shadow slowly across it.   1920

122

Let me be in your service
like the others
mumbling predictions,
mouth dry with jealousy.
Parched tongue
thirsting, not even for the word—
for me the dry air is empty
again without you.

I'm not jealous any more
but I want you.
I carry myself like a victim
to the hangman.
I will not call you
either joy or love.
All my own blood is gone.
Something strange paces there now.

Another moment
and I will tell you:
it's not joy but torture
you give me.
I'm drawn to you
as to a crime—
to your ragged mouth,
to the soft bitten cherry.

Come back to me,
I'm frightened without you.
Never had you such power
over me as now.
Everything I desire
appears to me.
I'm not jealous any more.
I'm calling you.   1920

123

A ring of shades danced on the springing meadow.
I threw among them a name like a song.
Everything melted. Only a mist
of sound remained with me.

I thought first that the name was one of the seraphim,
I was shy of bodies however light.
A few days and we flowed together;
I melted into a beloved shade.

Wild fruit falls again from the apple tree
and the image drifts by me like mist,
with curses for heaven and for itself,
still swallowing embers of jealousy.

And happiness rolls on like a gold hoop
someone else is guiding.
Spring drifts away and you chase it
waving your hand like a knife.

As it is we never emerge from the dance,
from the ring, from the enchantment.
Earth, the virgin, springs up again
in hills, but the mist hides them from us.   1920

FROM *POEMS* (1928)

CONCERT AT THE RAILWAY STATION

Can't breathe. And the firmament seething with worms,
and not one star speaking.
But as God's our witness, there's music above us—
the Aeonian maids, at whose song the station trembles,
and again the violin-laden air is sundered
and fused together by the whistles of trains.

Immense park. The station a glass sphere.
A spell cast again on the iron world.
The train carriage is borne away in state
to the echoing feast in misty Elysium.
Peacocks crying, a piano's bass notes—
I'm late. I'm afraid. This is a dream.

And I enter the station, the glass forest.
The harmony of violins is dishevelled and weeping.
The savage life of the night choir,
a smell of roses from rotting beds,
where the beloved shade passed the night
under the glass sky, among the travelling crowds.

And I think, how like a beggar the iron world
shivers, covered with music and froth.
And I go out through the glass passage. The steam
blinds the pupils of the violin bows. Where are you off to?
It's the funeral feast of the beloved shade.
It's the last time the music sounds for us.   1921

I was washing outside in the darkness,
the sky burning with rough stars,
and the starlight, salt on an axe-blade.
The cold overflows the barrel.

The gate's locked,
the land's grim as its conscience.
I don't think they'll find the new weaving,
finer than truth, anywhere.

Star-salt is melting in the barrel,
icy water is turning blacker,
death's growing purer, misfortune saltier,
the earth's moving nearer to truth and to dread.   1921

To some winter is nut-stains and blue-eyed punch,
to some, wine fragrant with cinnamon, and to some
it's a salt of commands from the cruel stars
to carry into a smoky hut.

The warm droppings of a few hens
and a tepid muddle of sheep.
For life, for life and care, I'll give up everything.
A kitchen match could keep me warm.

Look, all I have with me is a clay pot
and the twitterings of the stars in my thin ears.
I can't help loving through unfledged bird skin
the yellow of grass, warmth of the black earth.

To smoothe out fur and turn straw in silence,
and hunger like an apple tree wrapped against winter,
stupidly, and thirst for another
and touch nothing in the dark, and wait.

Well may the conspirators hurry over the frail
creaking snow-crust like a flock of sheep. To some, winter
is wormwood, and bitter smoke as the tents are pitched,
to others, a sheet of salt ready to fall.

O if I could hoist a lantern on a long pole
and be led by a dog, under the salt of stars,
with a rooster in a pot, to the fortune-teller's yard.
But the white of the snow eats the eyes to the quick.   1922

129

The scalp tingles with cold.
Nobody speaks out.
Time pares me away
like the heel of your shoe.

Life overcomes life.
The sound fades out.
Something is always missing.
There's no time to remember it.

You know, it was better before.
But there's no comparing
how the blood used to whisper
and how it whispers.

It's plain that some purpose
is moving these lips.
The tree-top laughs and plays
into the day of the axes.   1922

No way of knowing
when this song began.
Does the thief rustle to its tune? ....
Does the prince of mosquitoes hum it?

O, if I could speak once more
about nothing at all,
blaze up like a struck match,
nudge night awake with my shoulder,

heave up the smothering haystack,
the muffling hat of air,
shake out the stitches
of the sack of caraway seeds,

then the pink knot of blood,
the hushing of these dry grasses
would be here in their trance after
a century, a hayloft, a dream.   1922

I climbed the ladder leaning against the hay,
into the uncombed loft.
I breathed the haydust of milky stars.
I breathed the matted scurf of space.

And I thought, why stir up the swarm
of long drawn-out lines of sound?
Why imprison the miraculous Aeolian harmony
in this ceaseless squabble?

The Great Bear, the dipper, has seven stars.
On earth there are five good senses.
The darkness swells and rings out,
and swells and rings out again.

The huge unhitched load sticks up
on top of the universe,
and soon the hayloft, the old chaos,
will itch and swirl with dust.

We rustle fish-scales that are not ours.
We sing against the fur of the world.
We string a lyre, as though we could not wait
for the shaggy fleece to grow over us.

Mowers bring back the goldfinches
that have fallen from their nests.
I will burst out of these burning lines
and return to the phrase of sound where I was born,

so that the pink link of blood
and the one-armed ringing of the grass may pronounce
their last good-byes: the one mustering courage,
the other setting out for its dream beyond reason.   1922

133

The wind brought comfort to us.
We could feel in the azure
dragonflies with Assyrian wings,
vibrations of the noded dark.

And the darkened sky's underside
threatened like the thunder of armies,
forest of mica membranes
flying with six-armed bodies.

There is a blind niche in the azure:
in each blessed noon
one fateful star trembles,
hinting at the depth of night.

And Azrael, among scales of crippled wings
threading his difficult way,
takes by its high arm
the defeated sky.   1922

l.13: Azrael, in Jewish and Mohammedan angelology, is the angel of death.

135

THE AGE

My animal, my age, who will ever be able
to look into your eyes?
Who will ever glue back together the vertebrae
of two centuries with his blood?
Blood the maker gushes
from the throats of the things of earth.
Already the hanger-on is trembling
on the sills of days to come.

Blood the maker gushes
from the throats of the things of earth
and flings onto a beach like a burning fish
a hot sand of sea-bones,
and down from the high bird-net,
out of the wet blocks of sky
it pours, pours, heedlessly
over your death-wound.

Only a metal the flute has melted
will link up the strings of days
until a time is torn out of jail
and the world starts new.
The age is rocking the wave
with human grief
to a golden beat, and an adder
is breathing in time with it in the grass.

44

The buds will go on swelling,
the rush of green will explode,
but your spine has been shattered,
my splendid derelict, my age.
Cruel and feeble, you'll look back
with the smile of a half-wit:
an animal that could run once,
staring at his own tracks.   1923

The original second stanza of this poem was cancelled by Mandelstam and
replaced by the lines that serve as the basis of this translation on 3 February
1936—C.B.

136

HE WHO FINDS A HORSESHOE

We look at the forest and we say
here are many ships already in the trees, masts,
the red pines
bare of their rough burden clear to the top,
they should creak in the storm
like solitary pines,
in the raging treeless air.
The plumbline fixed
to the dancing deck, under the wind's salt heel,
will hold fast, as the sea-farer,
with unbridled thirst for distance, trawls
through the furrows of water the geometer's
frail instruments, tracing
against the pull of the bosom of the earth
the rough surfaces of the seas.

And breathing the smell of the tears
of resin that seep from the ship's timbers,
gazing lovingly upon
the rivetted boards fitted into bulkheads
(not by the peaceable Bethlehem carpenter
but by that other, the father
of wanderings, the sea-farer's friend)
we say
these too once stood on the earth,
uncomfortable as a donkey's spine,
their tops forgetting their roots,
on a famous mountain,
and sighed under the sweet pouring rain,
and in vain offered to heaven their noble burden
for a pinch of salt.

Where to start?
Everything cracks and shakes.
The air trembles with similes.
No one word's better than another;
the earth moans with metaphors,
and the shays hitched to shimmering flocks
of birds all heaving together
fly apart, racing
against the day's favorites.

Thrice blessed is he who puts a name in his song.
The song graced with a name
outlives the others.
She may be known among her companions by her headband
that preserves her from fainting, from too-strong numbing
        odors
whether of the nearness of man,
the fur of a powerful animal, or simply
the smell of savory rubbed between hands.

Sometimes the air is dark as water, and everything in it
is swimming like a fish,
fanning its way through the sphere,
through the dense, yielding, scarcely warm
crystal with wheels moving in it, and horses shying,
and Neaera's damp black earth, that is turned up afresh
every night by forks, tridents, mattocks, plows.
The air is as deeply mingled as the earth;
you can't get out of it, and it's hard to get in.

A rustling runs through the trees as through a lush meadow.
Children play jacks with bits of animals' backbones.
The frail tally of our age is almost done.
For what there was, thank you.
For my part, I made mistakes, got lost,
came out wrong. The age clanged like a golden ball,
hollow, seamless, held by no one.
When it was touched it answered 'yes' and 'no'
as a child answers
'I'll give you the apple', or 'I won't give you the apple',
with a face that matches the voice saying the words.

The sound is still ringing, though what caused it has gone.
The stallion is lying in a lather, in the dust, snorting,
but the tight arch of his neck recalls
the stretched legs racing,
not just the four of them
but as many as the stones on the road
coming alive by fours
at each bound of the fiery pacer.

Therefore
the one who finds a horseshoe
blows the dust from it,
rubs it with wool till it shines,
and then
hangs it over the door
to rest,
not to be made to strike sparks from the flint again.
Human lips
      that have no more to say
keep the shape of the last word they said,
and the hand goes on feeling the full weight
even after the jug
      has splashed itself half empty
            on the way home.

What I'm saying now isn't said by me.
It's dug out of the ground like grains of petrified wheat.
Some portray
      a lion on their coins,
others
      a head;
all sorts of round bits of brass, gold, bronze
lie in the earth sharing the same honor.
The age tried to bite through them, leaving its teethmarks.
Time gnaws at me like a coin,
and there's not even enough of me left for myself.

Moscow. 1923

l.53: Neaera is a name often used by classical poets for 'sweetheart'. Cf. Milton's 'the tangles of Neaera's hair' in *Lycidas*.

THE SLATE ODE

Two stars coming together—a great meeting,
a flint path from an old song,
the speech of flint and air,
flint and water, a ring with a horseshoe;
on the layered rock of the clouds
a milky sketch in slate—
not the schooldays of worlds
but the woolly visions of light sleep.

We sleep upright in the thick night
under the fleece hat.
The spring runs back whispering into the timbers
like a little chain, little warbler, speech.
Terror and Split write with the same little stick of milk.
Here, taking form, is the first draft
of the students of running water.

Steep goat cities.
The massive layering of flint.
And still the beds,
the sheep churches, the villages.
In the plumbline is their sermon,
in the water their lesson, time wears them fine,
and the transparent forest of the air
has been filled with them for a long time.

Like a dead hornet by the honey-comb
the pied day is swept out in disgrace.
The black night-harrier carries
burning chalk to feed the flint.
To erase day by day the writings
from the iconoclastic board,
and to shake visions, already transparent,
out of the hand like nestlings.

The fruit was coming to a head. The grapes ripening,
the day raging as a day rages.
Knucklebones—a gentle game—
and the coats of savage sheep-dogs, at noon.
Like rubble from icy heights,
from the backs of green icons,
the famished water flows, eddying,
playing like the young of an animal,

and crawls toward me like a spider,
over the moon-splashed crossings.
I hear the slate screech
on the startled crag.
Memory, are those your voices
teaching, splitting the night,
tossing slates into the forests,
ripping them from the beaks of birds?

Only the voice will teach us
what was clawing and fighting there.
And we will guide the callous slate
as the voice leads us.
I break the night, burning chalk
for the firm notation of a moment.
I exchange noise for the singing of arrows.
I exchange order for the fierce drumming of a grouse.

Who am I? No simple mason,
roofer or boatman.
I'm a double-dealer, with a double soul.
I'm the friend of night, the assassin of day.
Blessed is he who called the flint
the student of running water.
And blessed is he who buckled
the feet of the mountains onto solid ground.

Now I study the scratched diary
of the slate's summer,
the language of flint and air,
a layer of darkness, a layer of light.
I want to thrust my hand
into the flint path from an old song
as into a wound, and hold together
the flint and the water, the horseshoe and the ring.

1923

140

1 JANUARY 1924

Whoever kisses time's ancient nodding head
will remember later, like a loving son,
how the old man lay down to sleep
in the drift of wheat outside the window.
He who has opened the eyes of the age,
two large sleepy apples with inflamed lids,
hears forever after the roar of rivers
swollen with the wasted, lying times.

The age is a despot with two sleepy apples
to see with, and a splendid mouth of earth.
When he dies he'll sink onto the numb
arm of his son, who's already senile.
I know the breath growing weaker by the day.
Not long now till the simple song
of the wrongs of earth is cut off,
and a tin seal put on the lips.

O life of earth! O dying age!
I'm afraid no one will understand you
but the man with the helpless smile
of one who has lost himself.
O the pain of peeling back the raw eyelids
to look for a lost word, and with lime
slaking in the veins, to hunt
for night herbs for a tribe of strangers!

The age. In the sick son's blood the deposit of lime
is hardening. Moscow's sleeping like a wooden coffin.
There's no escaping the tyrant century.
After all these years the snow still smells of apples.
I want to run away from my own doorstep,
but where? Out in the street it's dark,
and my conscience glitters ahead of me
like salt strewn on the pavement.

Somehow I've got myself set for a short journey
through the back lanes, past thatched eaves, starling houses,
an everyday passer-by, in a flimsy coat,
forever trying to button the lap-robe.
Street after street flashes past,
the frozen runners crunch like apples;
can't get the button through the button-hole,
it keeps slipping out of my fingers.

The winter night thunders
like iron hardware through the Moscow streets.
Knocks like a frozen fish, or billows in steam,
flashing like a carp in a rosy tea-room.
Moscow is Moscow again. I say hello to her.
'Don't be stern with me; never mind.
I still respect the brotherhood
of the deep frost, and the pike's justice.'

The pharmacy's raspberry globe shines onto the snow.
Somewhere an Underwood typewriter's rattled.
The sleigh-driver's back, the snow knee-deep,
what more do you want? They won't touch you, won't kill you.
Beautiful winter, and the goat sky
has crumbled into stars and is burning with milk.
And the lap-robe flaps and rings
like horse-hair against the frozen runners.

And the lanes smoked like kerosene stoves,
swallowed snow, raspberry, ice,
endlessly peeling, like a Soviet sonatina,
recalling nineteen-twenty.
The frost is smelling of apples again.
Could I ever betray to gossip-mongers
the great vow to the Fourth Estate
and oaths solemn enough for tears?

Who else will you kill? Who else will you worship?
What other lie will you dream up?
There's the Underwood's cartilage. Hurry, rip out a key,
you'll find a little bone of a pike.
And in the sick son's blood the deposit of lime
will melt, and there'll be sudden blessèd laughter.
But the simple sonatina of typewriters
is only a faint shade of those great sonatas.   1924

Stanza 8, Fourth Estate: traditionally, the press (as an additional estate of the
realm, after the Lords Spiritual, the Lords Temporal, and the Commons).
Mandelstam's 'vow' should be read as a vow to spiritual and intellectual in-
dependence.

141

No, I was no one's contemporary—ever.
That would have been above my station.
How I loathe that other with my name.
He certainly never was me.

The age is a despot with two sleepy apples
to see with, and a splendid mouth of earth.
When he dies he'll subside onto the numb
arm of his son, who's already ageing.

As the age was born I opened my red eyelids,
my eyes were large sleepy apples.
The rivers thundered, informing me
of the bloodshot lawsuits of men.

A hundred years back,
on the camp-bed, on a drift of pillows,
there was a sprawled clay body: the age
getting over its first drunk.

What a frail bed, when you think
how the world creaks on its journey.
Well, we can't forge another.
We'd better get along with this one.

In stuffy rooms, in cabs, in tents,
the age is dying. Afterwards
flames will flutter like feathers, on the apple-skins,
on the curled wafers of horn.

Stanza 2: cf. previous poem. It is common in Mandelstam's practice for the
material of one poem to recur in slightly altered (and sometimes in identical)
form in an adjacent or related poem.

POEMS OF THE THIRTIES

201

Don't say a word to a soul.
Forget all you've seen,
bird, old woman, cage,
and the rest.

Or else at break of day
the moment you open your mouth,
you'll start to shiver
like the needles of a pine.

You'll see the wasp at the cottage,
pencil-case, ink stains,
blueberries ungathered
in those woods.

Tiflis. October 1930

202

Much we have to fear,
big-mouth beside me!

Our tobacco turns into dust,
nut-cracker, friend, idiot!

And I could have whistled through life like a starling,
eating nut pies . . . .

but clearly there's no chance of that.

Tiflis. October 1930

LENINGRAD

I've come back to my city. These are my own old tears,
my own little veins, the swollen glands of my childhood.

So you're back. Open wide. Swallow
the fish-oil from the river lamps of Leningrad.

Open your eyes. Do you know this December day,
the egg-yolk with the deadly tar beaten into it?

Petersburg! I don't want to die yet!
You know my telephone numbers.

Petersburg! I've still got the addresses:
I can look up dead voices.

I live on back stairs, and the bell,
torn out nerves and all, jangles in my temples.

And I wait till morning for guests that I love,
and rattle the door in its chains.

Leningrad. December 1930

222

I saw the world of power through a child's eyes—
oysters frightened me, I looked bashfully at the sentries—
I owe it not one jot of my soul:
something alien to me, which I never wanted.

I never stood under the bank's Egyptian porch,
stupidly pompous, in a beaver mitre, glowering.
Never, never, above the lemon Neva, to the rustle
of hundred rouble notes, did a gypsy girl dance for me.

Feeling executions on the way, I escaped from the roar
of rebellious events, to the Nereids on the Black Sea,
and from those days' beautiful women, gentle European women,
what anguish I consumed, what torment!

Why then does this city, even now, satisfy
my thoughts and my feelings at home in its ancient night?
It is more insolent than ever with its frost and fires,
more arrogant, damned, empty—it looks younger.

Maybe that's because, in a child's picture book,
I saw Lady Godiva draped in her red mane,
and I'm still whispering under my breath
Good-bye, Lady Godiva . . . Godiva, I've forgotten . . .

January 1931

Nereids: sea-nymphs, daughters of the ancient sea god Nereus.

223

O Lord, help me to live through this night—
I'm in terror for my life, your slave:
to live in Petersburg is to sleep in a grave.

January 1931

224

You and I will sit for a while in the kitchen,
the good smell of kerosene,

sharp knife, big round loaf—
Pump up the stove all the way.

And have some string handy
for the basket, before daylight,

to take to the station
where no one can come after us.

Leningrad. January 1931

After midnight the heart picks the locked silence
right out of your hands. Then it may remain
quiet, or it may raise the roof.
Like it or not, it's the only one of its kind.

Like it or not, you may know it but you'll never catch it,
so why shiver, now, like a thrown-out child?
After midnight the heart has its banquet,
gnawing on a silvery mouse.

Moscow. March 1931

227

For the sake of the future's trumpeting heroics,
for that exalted tribe,
I was robbed of my cup at my fathers' feast,
and of my laughter and honor.

The wolfhound age springs at my shoulders
though I'm no wolf by blood.
Better to be stuffed up a sleeve like a fleece cap
in a fur coat from the steppes of Siberia,

and so not see the snivelling, nor the sickly smears,
nor the bloody bones on the wheel,
so all night the blue foxes would still gleam
for me as they did in the first times.

Lead me into the night by the Yenesey
where the pine touches the star.
I'm no wolf by blood,
and only my own kind will kill me.

17–28 March 1931

229

My eyelashes are pins. In my chest one tear is boiling.
I'm not frightened to know that the storm will go on and on.
Some ghoul tries to hurry me, make me forget,
but even when I can't breathe I want to live till I die.

Hearing something, sitting up on the boards,
I look around wildly, still half asleep.
It's a prisoner intoning a rough song, at the hour
when dawn draws the first thread, outside the jail.

Moscow. March 1931

230

Outside the window, the darkness.
After me, the deluge.
Then what? The town snoring,
a mob in the cloak-room.

Masked ball. Wolfhound century.
Don't forget it.
Keep out of sight, a cap in a sleeve,
and God preserve you!

Moscow. March 1931

232

No, it's not for me to duck out of the mess
behind the cabdriver's back that's Moscow.
I'm the cherry swinging from the streetcar strap
of an evil time. What am I doing alive?

We'll take Streetcar A and then Streetcar B,
you and I, to see who dies first. As for Moscow,
one minute she's a crouched sparrow,
the next she's puffed up like a pastry—

how does she find time to threaten from holes?
You do as you please, I won't chance it.
My glove's not warm enough for the drive
around the whole whore Moscow.

April 1931

235

To Anna Akhmatova

Keep my words forever for their aftertaste of misfortune and
    smoke,
their tar of mutual tolerance, honest tar of work.
Sweet and black should be the water of Novgorod wells
to reflect the seven fins of the Christmas star.

And in return, father, friend, rough helper, I
the unrecognized brother, outlawed from the people's family,
promise to fit the beam-cages tight to the wells
so the Tartars can lower the princes in tubs, for torture.

O ancient headsman's blocks, keep on loving me!
Players in the garden seem to aim at death, and hit nine-pins.
I walk through my life aiming like that, in my iron shirt
(why not?) and I'll find an old beheading axe in the woods.

Khmelnitskaya. 3 May 1931

LAMARCK

There was an old man shy as a boy,
a gawky, timid patriarch—
who picked up the challenge for the honor of nature?
Who else? The man of passion, Lamarck.

If all that's alive is no more than a blot
for the brief escheated day,
give me the last rung
on Lamarck's moving ladder.

I'll hiss my way down through the lizards and snakes
to the annelid worms and the sea-slugs,
across resilient gangways, through valleys,
I'll shrink, and vanish, like Proteus.

I'll put on a shell cloak,
I'll be done with warm blood,
I'll grow suckers, I'll sink feelers
into the foam of the sea.

We went through the classes of insects
with their liquid liqueur-glass eyes.
He said, 'Nature's a shambles.
There's no vision. You're seeing for the last time.'

He said, 'No more harmony.
In vain you loved Mozart.
Now comes the deafness of spiders.
Here is ruin stronger than our strength.

Nature has gone away from us
as though she didn't need us.
She's slid the oblong brain
into a dark sheath, like a sword.

She's forgotten the drawbridge.
She lowered it late
for those with a green grave,
red breath, sinuous laughter . . .'   7–9 May 1932

BATYUSHKOV

An idler with a wand for a walking stick,
gentle Batyushkov lives with me,
strides down the alleys into Zamost'e,
sniffs a rose, sings Zafna—

nothing has ever been lost!
I believe I bowed when I met him,
and pressed his pale cold glove
like a man with a fever.

He smiled a little, I pronounced Thank you,
too shy to say any more.
No one else could trace those sounds,
no other waves sound the same.

He was bringing with him our anguish
and our great richness, and he was muttering:
the noise of making a poem, the bell of brotherhood,
the soft patter of tears,

still mourning for Tasso. And he answered me
'I can't get a taste for praise.
Only the grape-flesh of poetry
ever cooled my tongue.'

You that live in cities with city friends
would scarcely believe it:
eternal dreams, blood samples
pouring from one glass to the next.

Moscow. 18 June 1932

Konstantine Nikolaevich Batyushkov (1787–1855), a contemporary of Pushkin,
was one of the greatest of Russian poets. 'The Dying Tasso' is among his best
known poems. The name Zafna occurs in his poem 'Istochnik' (The Spring),
1810. Zamost'e is a town to the south-east of Lublin.

TO THE GERMAN LANGUAGE

Destroying myself, contradicting myself,
like the moth flying into the midnight flame,
suddenly all that binds me to our language
tempts me to leave it.

What is there between us? Praise without flattery.
Unfeigned friendship, face to face.
Let an alien family, to our west,
teach us seriousness and honor.

Poetry, you put storms to good use.
I remember a German officer,
his sword hilt wrapped with roses
and Ceres on his lips.

Already, in Frankfurt, the fathers were yawning,
and no one had yet heard of Goethe,
they were writing hymns, stallions were prancing
in their places, like letters of the alphabet.

Friends, tell me, in what Valhalla
did we crack nuts together, you and I?
What freedom was ours to spend as we pleased,
what landmarks did you leave for me?

And we ran straight from the first-rate newness
of a page of an almanac
down shallow steps, unafraid, into the grave,
as into a cellar to draw a jug of Moselle.

An alien language will be my swaddling clothes.
Long before I dared to be born
I was a letter of the alphabet, a verse like a vine,
I was the book that you all see in dreams.

When I was asleep and without feature
friendship woke me like a shot.
Nightingale-god, let Pylades' fate be mine,
or tear my tongue out, for it's no use to me.

Nightingale-god, I'm being conscripted still
for new plagues, for seven-year massacres.
Sound has shrivelled, words are hoarse and rebellious,
but you're alive still, and with you I'm at peace.

8–12 August 1932

267

ARIOSTO

Ariosto—no one in Italy more delightful—
these days has a frog in his throat.
He amuses himself with the names of fish,
he rains nonsense into the seas.

Like a musician with ten cymbals,
forever breaking in on his own music,
he leads us backwards and forwards, himself quite lost
in the maze of chivalric scandals.

A Pushkin in the language of the cicadas,
with a Mediterranean haughtiness to his melancholy,
he leaves his hero struggling with the preposterous,
and shudders, and is another man.

He says to the sea: roar but don't think!
To the maiden on the rock: lie there without bedclothes!
We've heard too little—tell us again,
while there's blood in the veins, and a roar in the ears.

O lizard city with a crust for a heart, and no soul,
Ferrara, give birth to more of such men!
While there's blood in the veins, hurry, tell the story
so often told, once more from the beginning.

It's cold in Europe. Italy is in darkness.
And power—it's like having to swallow a barber's hand.
But he goes on improving his act, playing
the great man smiling out of the window

at the lamb on the hill, the monk on his donkey,
the Duke's men-at-arms silly with wine
and the plague and garlic,
the baby dozing under a net of flies.

I love his desperate leisure,
his babble, the salt and sugar of his words,
the sounds happily conspiring in twos and threes.
Why should I want to split the pearl?

Ariosto, maybe this age will vanish
and we'll pour your azure and our Black Sea together
into one wide fraternal blue.
We too know it well. We've drunk mead on its shore.

Stary Krym. 4–6 May 1933

271

Cold spring, in starving Stary Krym,
still with its guilt, as it was under Wrangel.
Sheep-dogs in the courtyard, patches on the rags,
even the acrid smoke is the same.

And the empty distance as good as ever.
The trees with buds starting to swell
stand like shy strangers. The almond's pitiful,
decked out in yesterday's silliness.

Nature wouldn't know her own face.
From the Ukraine, the Kuban, terrible ghosts.
And the famished peasants, in felt shoes,
stand guard at their gates, never touching the rings.

Stary Krym. May 1933

Stary Krym: a small town in the Crimea, once its capital, where the Mandelstams
lived for a time during the terrible famine of 1932–33.

272

The apartment's dumb as paper,
it emptied by itself.
Sounds start slithering
through the radiator.

Our estate's in order:
telephone frozen into frog,
all our veteran possessions
homesick for the street.

A damnation of flimsy walls.
Nowhere to run to.
I'll have to play tunes on a comb
for somebody, like a clown.

Tunes ruder than students sing,
more insolent than young party members,
but I have to teach the hangmen,
perched on their school-bench, bird-notes.

I read ration-books.
I catch phrases like nooses.
I sing warning lullabies
to the rich peasant's good child.

Someone who draws from the life,
some fine-comb of the flax collective,
someone with blood in his ink
ought to sit on this stake.

Some respected informer, left
like salt when a purge boiled away,
some family's breadwinner
ought to crush this moth.

What teeth of malice lurking
in every detail,
as though Nekrasov's hammer
were still nailing the nails.

Let's start as though we were stretched
on the headsman's block, you and I,
on the other side of seventy years.
Old loafer, it's time for you to stamp your boots.

It won't be the fountain Hippocrene
that will burst through the hack-work walls,
but the current of household terror
in this evil coop in Moscow.

Moscow, Furmanov pereulok. November 1933

Stanza 8: Nikolay Alexeevich Nekrasov (1821–1878), the great realist and 'civic'
poet of the mid-nineteenth century.

286

[THE STALIN EPIGRAM]

Our lives no longer feel ground under them.
At ten paces you can't hear our words.

But whenever there's a snatch of talk
it turns to the Kremlin mountaineer,

the ten thick worms his fingers,
his words like measures of weight,

the huge laughing cockroaches on his top lip,
the glitter of his boot-rims.

Ringed with a scum of chicken-necked bosses
he toys with the tributes of half-men.

One whistles, another meouws, a third snivels.
He pokes out his finger and he alone goes boom.

He forges decrees in a line like horseshoes,
One for the groin, one the forehead, temple, eye.

He rolls the executions on his tongue like berries.
He wishes he could hug them like big friends from home.

[November 1933]

This poem, when word of it reached the authorities, was the occasion of Mandelstam's first arrest (1934). See Introduction.

287

As a stream falls from a single crack in a glacier
and its taste has two faces, one forward
one backward, and one is sweet and one hard,

so I die for the last time through each moment of these days,
and one way the old sighing frees me no longer,
and the other way the goal can no longer be seen.

Moscow. December 1933

To the memory of Andrey Bely

Blue eyes, and the bone of the forehead glowing—
the venom of the world that renews its youth was your guide.

And for the great magic that was to be yours
you were never to judge, never to curse.

They crowned you with a divine dunce-cap,
turquoise teacher, torturer, tyrant, fool.

A Gogol-ghost exploded like a blizzard in Moscow,
whirling, dense, clear, and unknowable.

With your collection of space and diploma of feathers,
author, young goldfinch, student, little student, sleighbell,

ice-skater, first-born, the age hauled you by the scruff
through new cases of words, still asleep under the snow.

Often one writes 'execution' and pronounces it 'song'.
Some ailments simplicity may have stung to death.

But our minds don't go off with a popgun straightness.
It's not the paper but the news that saves us.

As dragonflies, missing the water, land in the reeds,
so the fat pencils settled into the dead man,

sheets were unfolded on knees for our glorious future,
and they drew, apologizing to every line.

Between you and the country a link of ice is forming,
so lie there and grow young, and never melt

and let those to come, the young, let them never inquire
what it's like for you lying there, orphan, in the clean void.

Moscow. 10 January 1934

Andrey Bely (1880–1934), whose real name was Bugaev, was one of the greatest
of the Russian Symbolists. He was buried on 10 January 1934 (see following poem).

10 JANUARY 1934

I am haunted by a few chance phrases,
repeating all day 'the rich oil of my sadness'.
O God how black are the dragonflies of death,
how blue their eyes, and how black is that blue!

Where is the rule of the first-born? Or the felicity of custom?
Or the tiny hawk that melts deep in the eyes?
Or learning? Or the bitter taste of stealth?
Or the firm outline? Or the straightness of speech

honestly weaving back and forth,
a skater into a blue flame,
his blades in the frosty air braiding
the clink of glasses in a glacier?

Ahead of him solutions of three-layered salts,
the voices of German wise men,
fifty years of the glittering disputes
of the Russian first-born, rose in half an hour.

Suddenly music leapt from ambush—
a tiger was hiding in the instruments—
not to be heard, not to soften a thing,
it moved in the name of the muscles, of the drumming
      forehead,

of the tender mask just removed,
of the plaster fingers holding no pen,
of the puffed lips, of the hardened caress,
of the crystallized calm and goodness.

The furs on the coats breathed. Shoulder pressed shoulder.
Health was a red ore boiling—blood, sweat.
Sleep in the jacket of sleep, that held once
a dream of moving half a step forward.

And there was an engraver in the crowd
proposing to transfer onto pure copper
what the draftsmen, blackening paper,
merely sketched in split hair.

So I may hang on my own eyelashes,
swelling, ripening, reading all the parts in the play
till I'm picked.
The plot is the one thing we know.

January 1934

293

To Andrey Bely

The ranges of the Caucasus followed his baton,
he tramped the paths of the packed Alps, waving his arms;
looking around him, he rushed as though frightened
through the chatter of an endless crowd.

He brought across—as only one with the power could
      have done—
a crowd of minds, events, impressions:
Rachel looked into the mirror of phenomena,
and Leah wore a wreath as she sang.

Moscow. January 1934

295

Seamstress of bewitching glances,
heir to delicate shoulders,
at last the rough male has gone under—
speech is the drowned woman rising without words.

Fish move between blazing fins,
gills puffing water. Now
they're yours, pronouncing their soundless 'o's.
Feed them the bread of your body.

But we're not fish lapped in gold.
Our nurse was warm:
the flesh with its frail ribs,
the eyes' moist hollow fire.

Those poppy-stamens, your eyebrow, mark a dangerous race.
I'm in love like a Turkish soldier
with the defenceless crescent—your lip
and its small red wings.

Dear Turkish woman, never be angry.
I'll be sewn up in a sack with you,
for you I'll swallow your dark words,
I'll fill with the shapeless water.

Maria, help of the overwhelmed,
one can't wait for death, one must sleep.
I'm standing at your threshold. Please
go away. Please go. Please stay.

Moscow. February 1934

296

Your thin shoulders are for turning red under whips,
turning red under whips, and flaming in the raw cold.

Your child's fingers are for lifting flatirons,
for lifting flatirons, and for knotting cords.

Your tender soles are for walking on broken glass,
walking on broken glass, across bloody sand.

And I'm for burning like a black candle lit for you,
for burning like a black candle that dare not pray.

1934

Nereids, my Nereids,
sobbing is food and drink to you—
the daughters of the Mediterranean wrong
take offense at my compassion.

March [1935?]

299

BLACK EARTH

Manured, blackened, worked to a fine tilth, combed
like a stallion's mane, stroked under the wide air,
all the loosened ridges cast up in a single choir,
the damp crumbs of my earth and my freedom!

In the first days of plowing it's so black it looks blue.
Here the labor without tools begins.
A thousand mounds of rumor plowed open—I see
the limits of this have no limits.

Yet the earth's a mistake, the back of an axe;
fall at her feet, she won't notice.
She pricks up our ears with her rotting flute,
freezes them with the wood-winds of her morning.

How good the fat earth feels on the plowshare.
How still the steppe, turned up to April.
Salutations, black earth. Courage. Keep the eye wide.
Be the dark speech of silence laboring.

Voronezh. April 1935

'Black earth' (for the Russian *chernozem*) refers to the belt of rich black soil that
stretches from the Carpathians and the Black Sea to the Altay Mountains.

Earphones, earphones, who turned me in,
I won't let you forget these nights exiled on the steppe,
the lees of a voice on the radio at midnight resounding
from loudspeakers in Red Square.

How's the subway these days? Don't tell. Anything.
Don't ask how the buds are swelling.
You strokes of the Kremlin clock,
speech of the void shrunken to a point.

Voronezh. April 1935

l.1: the Russian *naushniki* means literally 'ear-phones' and, figuratively, 'informers',
i.e. 'those who turn one in'.

—What street is this?
—Mandelstam Street.
—What the hell kind of name is that?
No matter which way you turn it
it comes out crooked.

—He wasn't a straight-edge exactly.
His morals resembled no lily.
And that's why this street (or rather,
to be honest, this sewer)
was given the name
of that Mandelstam.

Voronezh. April 1935

Now I lodge in the cabbage patches of the important.
A servant might come walking here out of an old song.
The factory winds work for nothing.
The road paved with brushwood runs into the distance.

At the edge of the steppe the plow has turned up night
bristling with a frost of tiny lights.
In the next room, in big boots,
the peeved landlord stomps and stomps

over the floor, the deck, the coffin-lids
warped into crusts.
Not much sleep under strange roofs
with my life far away.

Voronezh. April 1935

305

I have to live, even though I died twice
and the town went half mad on water.

How handsome it looks, how high in heart and cheekbone,
how good the fat slice of earth on the plowshare.

How still the steppe, turned over in April.
But the sky, the sky—your Michelangelo! [1935]

306

Now I'm dead in the grave with my lips moving
and every schoolboy repeating the words by heart.

The earth is rounder in Red Square than anywhere,
all one side of a hardened will.

The earth in Red Square is rounder than anywhere.
No one would think it was so light of heart

bending back all the way down to the rice growing
on the last day of the last slave on the globe.

Voronezh. May 1935

307

You took away all the oceans and all the room.
You gave me my shoe-size in earth with bars around it.
Where did it get you? Nowhere.
You left me my lips, and they shape words, even in silence.

Voronezh [1935]

308

How dark it gets along the Kama.
The cities kneel by the river on oaken knees.

Draped in cobwebs, beard with beard,
black firs and their reflections run back into their childhood.

The water leaned into fifty-two pairs of oars,
pushed them upstream, downstream, to Kazan and Cherdyn.

There I floated with a curtain across the window,
a curtain across the window, and the flame inside was my head.

And my wife was with me there five nights without sleeping,
five nights awake keeping an eye on the guards.

Voronezh. May 1935

After his first arrest, Mandelstam was exiled to the town of Cherdyn in the Urals.
With his wife by his side he made part of the journey there along the river Kama.

I left with the evergreen east in my eyes.
The Kama and its riches dragged at the buoy.

Let me cut the hill and its campfire into layers.
There'll be no time to grow forests.

Let me settle here, right here.
Some people live here. The Urals live on and on.

Let me take this mirror country lying on its back
and button a long coat over it and keep it warm.

Voronezh. May 1935

312

STANZAS

1 I don't want to pay down the last penny of my soul
among hothouse adolescents. I go to the world
as the single peasant goes to the collective
and I find the people good.

2 I'm for the Red Army style overcoat,
down to the heels, simple flat sleeves,
cut like a rain cloud over the Volga,
to hang full on the chest, one fold down the back,
no stuff wasted on double hems;
you can roll it up in the summer.

3 A damned seam, a foolishness,
came between us. Now let it be clear:
I have to live, breathing and bolshevescent.
I'll be better-looking before I die,
staying to play among the people.

4 When you think how I raced around
   in a seven-inch sweat, in dear old Cherdyn,
   among the bell-bottomed river smells,
   not stopping to watch the goat-squabbles—
   a rooster in the transparent summer night.
   Grub and spit, and something, and babble—and got
   the woodpecker off my back. One jump—then sane again.

5 And you my sister Moscow, how light you are,
   coming to meet your brother's plane
   before the first street-car bell.
   You are gentler than the sea, you tossed salad
   of wood, glass, milk.

6 Once my country talked with me,
   indulged me, scolded me a little, never read me.
   But when I grew up and was a witness
   she noticed me all at once, and like a lens
   set me alight with one flash from the Admiralty.

7 I have to live, breathing and bolshevescent,
   laboring with language, disobeying, I and one other.
   I hear the Arctic throbbing with Soviet pistons.
   I remember everything—the necks of German brothers,
   the gardener-executioner whose pastime
   was the Lorelei's lilac comb.

8 I'm not robbed blind, not desperate,
   just, only, merely, thrown.
   When my string's tuned tight as Igor's Song,
   when I get my breath back, you can hear
   in my voice the earth, my last weapon,
   the dry dampness of acres of black earth.

Voronezh. May–June 1935

Stanza 6: the Admiralty is one of the most notable buildings and the central focal point of St. Petersburg (Leningrad).
Stanza 8: the Song of Igor is the principal monument of early Russian Literature.

'No, it's not migraine, but hand me the menthol pencil—
neither art's languid invitation, nor the fireworks of space.'

Life began in a trough, with a damp lisping whisper,
and went on into the soft soot of kerosene.

Then at some dacha, in a green shagreen binding,
it suddenly blazed up in lilac flames, no one knew why.

'No, it's not migraine, but hand me the menthol pencil—
neither art's languid invitation, nor the fireworks of space.'

Later, with straining eyes, through stained glass, painfully,
I see the sky, a club threatening, and the earth, a red bald spot.

After that I forget. It seems to break off
With a faint smell of resin, and what must be rotten whale oil.

No, not migraine, but the cold of neuter space,
the sharp sound of gauze tearing, the rumble of the carbolic
    guitar.   Voronezh. 23 April–July 1935

320

I want to give back this dust I've borrowed,
not as the flour from a white butterfly;
I want this thinking body
this vertebrate, this burnt body
that once knew its length, to be changed
into a thoroughfare, a country.

The dark pine needles shout.
The wreaths deep as wells,

the hoops of red-flagged needles
leaning on the lathes of death,
'o''s from an alphabet,
prolong a time once loved, a life.

The latest recruits were carrying out
orders under the hardened sky.
Infantry passed, under their rifles—
so many silent exclamations.

Blue eyes, hazel eyes,
guns aimed at the air in thousands,
in confusion—men, men, men—
who will come after them?

Voronezh. 21 July 1935

324

My goldfinch, I'll cock my head;
together we'll look at the world:
the winter day jagged as stubble,
is it rough to your eye as to mine?

Tail, little black and yellow boat.
Head dipped in color past the beak.
Goldfinch, do you know you're a goldfinch,
do you know how much?

What's the atmosphere back of his forehead?
It's black, red, yellow, white.
He keeps an eye out both ways. Now he's stopped
looking—he's flown from between them!

Voronezh. December 1936

328

It's not I, it's not you—it's they
who've locked up all the word endings.
The air that makes flutes of the reeds is theirs.
Human lips are snails, happy
to be laden with their breathing.

They have no names. He who enters their cartilage
falls heir to their domains.

And to men, their living hearts,
wandering the split paths, turning,
the pleasures you tell of will all be theirs,
and the pain that drives them back and forth in tides.

Voronezh. 9–27 December 1936

329

Today is all beak and no feathers
and it's staying that way. Why?
And a gate by the sea gazes at me
out of anchors and fogs.

Quietly, quietly warships are gliding
through faded water,
and in canals gaunt as pencils
under the ice the leads go on blackening.

Voronezh. 9–28 December 1936

The idol is motionless inside the hill,
an endless serenity in the ordered rooms.
Drops of oil strung round his neck
watch over the tides of sleep.

When he was a boy with a tame peacock
they gave him a rainbow to eat
and milk in clay roses
and they surrounded him with scarlet.

Now every bone is tied in a trance.
The knees are a man's, the shoulders and arms are a man's.
The whole of his mouth is a smile.
Thinking bone by bone, feeling with his forehead,
laboriously he resurrects what it was to be human.

Voronezh. December 1936

341

Mounds of human heads are wandering into the distance.
I dwindle among them. Nobody sees me. But in books
much loved, and in children's games I shall rise
from the dead to say the sun is shining.   [1936–1937?]

343

Dead poet with a ring for a name,
I'm near you, and I'm ringed too, like a falcon.
No messenger comes for me.
There's no step up to my door.

There's a forest of pines, of ink,
chained to my leg.
The horizon lies open, messenger
of no message.

The little mounds straggle on the steppe—
nomads. And the camps of the nights
keep moving on, the little nights
keep moving, leading their blind men.

Voronezh. 1–9 January 1937

344

When the sorcerer sets
the colors of horses
to whispering
in the sagging boughs,

the faded lazy hero,
bullfinch in winter,
small but strong,
is not in the mood for song.

The sky will lean out and over.
Under its raised brows I'll hurry
to my seat
in the lilac sleigh of the dead.

Voronezh. 6–10 January 1937

From what bleeding veins of ore
will the dear yeast of the world return to me
the accents, tears, labors,
the seething murmur of trouble,
all the lost sounds?

In my beggar's mind, for the first time,
ditches open, full of brassy water,
and I follow them away from myself,
loathing each step, unknown to myself,
both the blind man and his guide.

Voronezh. 12–18 January 1937

A little imp in wet fur
has crawled—well, where could he go—
into the thimbles under the hooves,
into the rushing tracks.
Kopeck by kopeck the seven-league air
picks the village bare.

The road splashes in the mirrors.
The rushing tracks
will stay there a while
with no shroud or mica.
The wheel beats at an angle.
Given up. Things could be worse.

I'm bored. My true work
babbles away, off the track.
Some other's come from the side,
and mocked, and knocked the axle crooked.

Voronezh. 12–18 January 1937

I am alone staring into the eye of the ice.
He is going nowhere. I came from there.
A miracle: the plain ironed to the end
of time, pleated without a wrinkle, is breathing.

The sun squints, a starched pauper;
calm grimace, source of calm.
The forests stretch to ten figures, almost complete.
The eyes bite on virgin bread, on snow.

Voronezh. 16 January 1937

350

What can we do with the plains' beaten weight?
No one can believe the slow hunger in them.
We think it's theirs, the vast flatness, but on the journey
to sleep, there it is in ourselves, there it is.

Farther and farther the question spreads—where are they going
and coming from? And crawling across them
is that not the one whose name we shriek in our sleep—
the Judas of nations unborn?

Voronezh. 16 January 1937

351

Oh the horizon steals my breath and takes it nowhere—
I'm choked with space!
I get my breath back, there's the horizon again.
I want something to cover my eyes.

I'd have liked the sand better—a life in layers
along the sawing shores of the river.
I'd have clung to the sleeves of the shy current,
to eddies, hollows, shallows.

We'd have worked well together, for a moment,
a century. I've wanted rapids like those.
I'd have laid my ear under the bark of drifting logs
to hear the rings marching outward.

Voronezh. 16 January 1937

353

What has held out against oxidation
and adulteration, burns like feminine silver,
and quiet labor silvers the iron plow
and the poet's voice.　　　　　　Voronezh. [1937]

354a

You're still alive, you're not alone yet—
she's still beside you, with her empty hands,
and a joy reaches you both across immense plains
through mists and hunger and flying snow.

Opulent poverty, regal indigence!
Live in it calmly, be at peace.
Blessed are these days, these nights,
and innocent is the labor's singing sweetness.

Miserable is the man who runs from a dog
in his shadow, whom a wind reaps at the knees,
and poor the one who holds out his rag of life
to beg mercy of a shadow.

Voronezh. January 1937

Now I'm in the spider-web of light.
The people with all the shadows of their hair
need light and the pale blue air
and bread, and snow from the peak of Elbrus.

And there's no one I can ask about it.
Alone, where would I look?
These clear stones weeping themselves
come from no mountains of ours.

The people need poetry that will be their own secret
to keep them awake forever,
and bathe them in the bright-haired wave
of its breathing.

Voronezh. 19 January 1937

Stanza 1: Elbrus is the highest mountain in the main range of the Caucasus.

357

Once a line of verse, in disgrace, father unknown,
fell from the sky like a stone, waking the earth somewhere.
No supplication can alter the poet's invention.
It can only be what it is. No one will judge it.

Voronezh. 20 January 1937

358

I hear, I hear the first ice
rustling under the bridges,
and I think of drunkenness swimming
radiant above our heads.

From stagnant stairs, from squares
flanked with jagged palaces
Dante's exhausted lips
more resonantly sang
his circling Florence.

So my shade with its eyes
gnaws the grains of that granite
and at night sees a hill of logs
that by day had seemed to be houses.

My shade twirls its thumbs, or yawns,
when there's no one but us,

or it kicks up a din, in company,
warmed by their wine and their sky,

and flings sour bread
to the importunate swans.

Voronezh. 21–22 January 1937

360

What shall I do with myself, now it's January?
The gaping city staggers and clings.
I think it's the locked doors that have made me drunk.
I could howl out of every lock and paper-clip.

The stocking-lanes barking,
knitted streets of junk-rooms,
idiots ducking into corners
to jump out of them—

in the pit, in the warty darkness,
I'm slipping toward the frozen pump-house.
I fall over my feet. I swallow dead air.
A fever of crows explodes.

90

And after that, there I am, gasping,
drumming on an icy wooden tub:
'Somebody read me! Somebody lead me! Somebody heal me!
Somebody say something on the jagged stairs!'

Voronezh. January–February 1937

364

I've gone, like the martyr of light and shade,
like Rembrandt, into a growing numbness of time.
One of my ribs is a burning blade,
but it's not in the keeping of these watchmen
nor of this soldier asleep under the storm.

Sir, magnificent brother, master
of the black-green darkness, may you forgive me:
the eye of the falcon-quill pen
and the hot casks in the midnight harem
waken, but waken to no good
the tribe frightened by furs in the twilight.

Voronezh. 8 February 1937

365

I sing from a wet throat and a dry soul,
vision properly moist, a mind behaving itself.
Is wine good for a man? Are furs
and the blood heaving with all that is Colchis?
But something is clenched in my chest. There's a hush there.
No language.
It's no longer me singing, it's my breath.
And my hearing's sheathed in a mountain. My head is deaf.

91

A selfless song is its own praise.
A comfort for friends, and for enemies, pitch.

A selfless song growing out of moss,
the one-voiced gift from the hunter's life,
which they sing riding the heights on horses,
with breath honest and open,
in honor and sternness caring only
to bring the young pair sinless to their wedding.

Voronezh. 8 February 1937

366

Sunderings of round bays, the gravel, the blue,
and the slow sail turning at last into a cloud—
almost before I prized you I was taken from you.
Longer than organ fugues, and bitter, is the sea grass,
pretending to be hair, and smelling of the long lie.
My head is awash with an iron tenderness.
Rust is nibbling along the gradual shore. . . .
Why was this different sand put under my head?

O guttural Urals, broad-shouldered lands of the Volga,
wide plains facing me—all my rights are there,
and I must still fill my lungs with them.

Voronezh. 8 February 1937

367

Armed with the sight of the fine wasps
sucking at the earth's axis, the earth's axis,
I recall each thing that I've had to meet,
I remember it by heart, and in vain.

I do not draw or sing
or ply the dark-voiced bow.
I make a little hole in life. How I envy
the strength and cunning of the wasps!

Oh if only once the sting of the air and the heat
of summer could make me hear
beyond sleep and death
the earth's axis, the earth's axis.

Voronezh. 8 February 1937

375

On a board of raspberry and pure gold,
on the side of Deep Saddle-Bow Mountain,
monstrous under drifted snow,
the sleigh-tracked, sleepy, horse-drawn
half town half river-bank, hitched up
in a harness of red coals, heated
with yellow resin burnt down to a sugar-tar,
was carried away.

Do not hunt here for the heaven of burnt oils
or the ice-skating Flemish brush-stroke.

There's no merry, gnarled, gnomish flock
in ear-flapped caps cawing here.

And do not trouble me with comparison,
but cut off my drawing that's in love with the long road,
like the maple bough, dry but still living,
which the smoke, running on stilts, carries away.

Voronezh. 6 March 1937

THE LAST SUPPER

The heaven of the supper fell in love with the wall.
It filled it with cracks. It fills them with light.
It fell into the wall. It shines out there
in the form of thirteen heads.

And that's my night sky, before me,
and I'm the child standing under it,
my back getting cold, an ache in my eyes,
and the wall-battering heaven battering me.

At every blow of the battering ram
stars without eyes rain down,
new wounds in the last supper,
the unfinished mist on the wall.

                                    Voronezh. 9 March 1937

378

I've lost my way in the sky—now where?
Let the one with the sky nearest to him answer.
It was easier for Dante's nine fallen
discuses to ring.

You can't cut me off from life—it dreams
of killing and caressing at a turn of the same hand,
so an anguish from Florence still
fills the ears, the eyes, the sockets.

No, do not oppress my forehead
with the sharp green laurel.
Better to cleave my heart
into blue shards, ringing,

then when I die, keeping faith
to the last with the lovers,
every sky in my breast will echo,
ringing out, and up.

Voronezh. 9–19 March 1937

380

Maybe this is the beginning of madness.
Maybe it's your conscience:
a knot of life in which we are seized and known
and untied for existence.

So in cathedrals of crystals not found on earth
the prudent spider of light
draws the ribs apart and gathers them again
into one bundle.

And gathered together by one thin beam
the bundles of pure lines give thanks.
One day they will meet, they will assemble
like guests with the visors up,

and here on earth, not in heaven,
as in a house filled with music,
if only we don't offend them, or frighten them away.
How good to live to see it!

Forgive me for what I am saying.
Read it to me quietly, quietly.

Voronezh. 15 March 1937

WINEJUG

Bad debtor to an endless thirst,
wise pander of wine and water,
the young goats jump up around you
and the fruits are swelling to music.

The flutes shrill, they rail and shriek
because the black and red all around you
tell of ruin to come
and no one there to change it.

Voronezh. 21 March 1937

384

How I wish I could fly
where no one could see me,
behind the ray of light
leaving no trace.

But you—let the light encircle you.
That's the one happiness.
Learn from a star the meaning
of light.

If it's a ray, if it's light,
that's only because
the whisper and chatter of lovers
strengthen and warm it.

And I want to tell you
that I'm whispering,
I'm giving you to the ray,
little one, in whispers.

Voronezh. 23 March 1937

Just for its potters the dark blue island,
Crete, the lighthearted, is great. When the earth they baked
rings you can hear their genius.
Do you hear fins of dolphins beating deep in the earth?

Speak of this sea and it will rise
in the clay, to smile in its oven.
and the frigid power of the vessel
became half sea, half eye.

Blue island, give me back what is mine.
Flying Crete, give back my work to me.
Fill the baked vessel
from the breasts of the flowing goddess.

This was, and was sung, and turned blue
in days before Odysseus,
before food and drink
were called 'my,' 'mine'.

Grow strong again and shine
o star of ox-eyed heaven,
and you, flying-fish of chance,
and you, o water saying yes.

                                        Voronezh. March [1937]

387

As though the fame of its mint and iota
were never enough, the Greek flute,
free, following its instincts,
matured, labored, crossed ditches.

No one can escape it,
nor quiet it, through clenched teeth,
nor coax it into speech with the tongue,
nor shape it with the lips.

And peace will never come to the flutist.
He feels that he is alone.
He remembers moulding his native sea
out of lilac clays, long ago.

With a sonorous climbing whisper,
with the patter of lips remembering,
he hurries to be thrifty,
he selects sounds, a neat miser.

When he's gone, we'll have no one
to knead lumps of clay to death.
When the sea filled me
my measure sickened me.

And in my own lips there's no peace.
'Mouther''s too close to 'murder'.
I let the flute's equinox
drop lower and lower.

Voronezh. 7 April 1937

388

I raise this green to my lips,
this muddy promise of leaves,
this forsworn earth,
mother of snowdrops and of every tree.

See how I'm blinded but strengthened,
surrendering to the least of the roots?
Are my eyes not blown out
by the exploding trees?

The little frogs are rolled up in their voices,
drops of mercury, huddled in a ball.
The twigs are turning into branches, and the fallow ground
is a mirage of milk.

Voronezh. 30 April 1937

393

Pear blossom and cherry blossom aim at me.
Their strength is crumbling but they never miss.

Stars in clusters of blossoms, leaves with stars—
what twin power is there? On what branch does truth blossom?

It fires into the air with flower or strength.
Its air-white full blossom-bludgeons put it to death.

And the twin scent's sweetness is unwelcoming.
It contends, it reaches out, it is mingled, it is sudden.

Voronezh. 4 May 1937

394

Limping like a clock on her left leg,
at the beloved gait, over the empty earth,
she keeps a little ahead of the quick girl,
her friend, and the young man almost her age.
What's holding her back
drives her on.
What she must know is coming
drags at her foot. She must know
that under the air, this spring,
our mother earth is ready for us
and that it will go on like this forever.

There are women with the dampness of the earth in their veins.
Every step they take there's a sobbing in a vault.
They were born to escort the dead, and be at the grave
first to greet those who rise again.
It would be terrible to want a caress from them
but to part with them is more than a man could do.
One day angel, next day the worm in the grave,
the day after that, a sketch.
What used to be within reach—out of reach.
Flowers never die. Heaven is whole.
But ahead of us we've only somebody's word.

Voronezh. 4 May 1937

395

Through Kiev, through the streets of the monster
some wife's trying to find her husband.
One time we knew that wife,
the wax cheeks, dry eyes.

Gypsies won't tell fortunes for beauties.
Here the concert hall has forgotten the instruments.
Dead horses along the main street.
The morgue smells in the nice part of town.

The Red Army trundled its wounded
out of town on the last street car,
one blood-stained overcoat calling,
'Don't worry, we'll be back!'

Voronezh. May 1937

CLARENCE BROWN

Clarence Brown is Professor of Russian Literature at Princeton University. He is the author of The Prose of Osip Mandelstam, *which offers translations of all that work, and of a biography,* Mandelstam, *published this year.*

W. S. MERWIN

W. S. Merwin's most recent books are Writings to an Unfinished Accompaniment, *a new book of poems, and* Asian Figures, *a group of proverbs, short poems and riddles from many Asian cultures. Both were published earlier this year.*